P9-DCW-668

101 "Answers" for New Teachers & Their Mentors

Effective Teaching Tips for Daily Classroom Use

Annette L. Breaux

EYE ON EDUCATION
6 DEPOT WAY WEST, SUITE 106
LARCHMONT, NY 10538
(914) 833–0551
(914) 833–0761 fax
www.eyeoneducation.com

Copyright © 2003 Eye On Education, Inc.
All Rights Reserved.

For information about permission to reproduce selections from this book, write: Eye On Education, Permissions Dept., Suite 106, 6 Depot Way West, Larchmont, NY 10538.

Library of Congress Cataloging-in-Publication Data

Breaux, Annette L.
  101 "answers" for new teachers and their mentors : effective teaching tips for daily classroom use / Annete L. Breaux
      p.   cm.
  ISBN 1–930556–48–9
  1. First year teachers—In-service training—Handbook, manuals, etc. 2. Mentoring in education—Handbook, manuals, etc. 3. Effective teaching—Handbook, manuals, etc. I. Title: One hundred and one "answers" for new teachers and their mentors. II. One hundred and one "answers" for new teachers and their mentors. III. Title.

  LB2844 .1.N4 B74 2003
  371.102—dc21

                                                                        2002029718

10 9 8 7 6 5 4 3

Editorial and production services provided by
Richard H. Adin Freelance Editorial Services
52 Oakwood Blvd., Poughkeepsie, NY 12603-4112
(845-471-3566)

Also Available from EYE ON EDUCATION

Coaching and Mentoring
First-Year and Student Teachers
India J. Podsen and Vicki Denmark

Teacher Retention:
What Is Your Weakest Link?
India J. Podsen

Handbook on Teacher Portfolios for
Evaluation and Professional Development
(Includes CD-ROM)
Pamela Tucker, James Stronge, and Christopher Gareis

Motivating and Inspiring Teachers:
The Educator's Guide for Building Staff Morale
Todd Whitaker, Beth Whitaker, and Dale Lumpa

Teaching Matters:
Motivating & Inspiring Yourself
Todd and Beth Whitaker

Dealing with Difficult Teachers, Second Edition
Todd Whitaker

Staff Development: Practices That Promote
Leadership in Learning Communities
Sally J. Zepeda

Instructional Supervision:
Applying Tools and Concepts
Sally J. Zepeda

Human Resources Administration:
A School-Based Perspective
Richard E. Smith

The Call to Teacher Leadership
Zepeda, Mayers, and Benson

Dedication

> *I dedicate this book to the memory of my grandfather, "Pop," the greatest teacher I will ever know.*

About the Author

Annette L. Breaux is one of the most entertaining and informative new authors and speakers in the field of education. She leaves her audiences with practical and doable techniques to implement in their classrooms immediately. Administrators agree that they see results from their teachers the next day.

Her message is one of practicality and personality in teaching, of feeling and healing in touching students' lives, and of common sense and creative teaching strategies. Her writings and presentations generate instant impact on the relationships between teachers and students.

A curriculum coordinator and former classroom teacher, she is also the director of the FIRST Program, an induction program for new teachers hailed as one of the best in the country. The program has been so successful in training and retaining new teachers that the Louisiana Department of Education has adopted it as a statewide model.

She recently teamed with Dr. Harry K. Wong to coauthor a book on new teacher induction. Her expertise is in student achievement, classroom management, and new teacher induction.

Her down-south warmth, infectious humor, and ability to touch the hearts and souls of educators invariably bring audiences to their feet. Teachers who have read Annette's writings or heard Annette speak agree that they walk away with user-friendly information, heartfelt inspiration, and a much-needed reminder that they truly have chosen the most noble of all professions—teaching.

Foreword

I conceived the idea for writing this book based on my experiences in working with and training mentors and new teachers. Interestingly, our school district, Lafourche Parish Schools (Thibodaux, Louisiana), had no real system of support for new teachers prior to 1996, and our attrition rate was right at 50 percent because of it. In 1996, based on the recommendations of Dr. Harry K. Wong, we implemented FIRST (Framework for Inducting, Retaining, and Supporting Teachers). Within one year, we saw a drastic decrease in our attrition rate, which now hovers at about 7 percent. Why this drastic difference? Because we were finally providing our new teachers with the support and training they so desperately needed and deserved. Successful teachers stay with a school district—not exactly rocket science! In fact, it wasn't long before the Louisiana Department of Education took notice of our successes with new teachers in Lafourche and adopted our induction program as a statewide model.

As part of a statewide mandate and an integral component of our induction process, all new teachers receive the support of a mentor for two years. As a member of the team that trains both mentors and new teachers, along with my experiences in training mentors and new teachers nationwide, I realized that many mentors receive basic training in mentoring techniques, but they find themselves at a loss regarding what to do with the new teachers on a daily basis. So, in developing this book, I went straight to the source and enlisted the support of mentors and new teachers. They used the suggestions in the book and found it was the missing link for which they had been searching. I also enlisted the support of seasoned teachers in order to get their feedback. You will see many of their comments throughout the book.

I share this book with you along with my love of children, my love of teaching, my belief that teachers touch lives, and my absolute conviction that every child is someone special.

It is my sincerest hope that you, too, will benefit from these 101 suggestions and teaching tips, because if you benefit, so will your students. Every child deserves a capable, competent, caring teacher. The children are our future, and, as teachers, we help to mold that future every single day.

Annette L. Breaux

Table of Contents

101 Effective Teaching Tips

Introduction

To the Teacher

Whether you are a brand-new first-time teacher or a seasoned veteran, you have chosen the most noble of all professions—teaching. Teaching is a highly skilled craft, requiring patience, commitment, dedication, a sincere love of children, charisma, confidence, and competence. By the very nature of your position as a teacher, you will affect the lives of each of your students on a daily basis.

If you are a new teacher, you know that it is your sincere desire to be successful, to inspire, to touch lives, and to make a difference. Yet, many of you, through no fault of your own, lack the necessary training to be effective from your very first day of teaching. Hopefully, you have signed on with a school district that provides induction training. Induction is a highly structured, systematic means of training and supporting new teachers beginning before their first day of teaching and continuing throughout their first two or three years. Mentoring is one vital component of the induction process. If you have not been assigned a mentor, find one. There are many capable, competent, caring teachers out there who are more than willing to share their expertise with novices. You cannot and will not be expected to know everything from day one. You'll need guidance. And although mentors cannot provide for all of the needs of new teachers, they can be valuable assets to you as you begin your career. So seek out the most positive, enthusiastic, successful teacher on the faculty and enlist his/her support in order to help ensure your success in the classroom from day one.

Remember, you are helping to mold the future, and your influence will long outlive you. You are a teacher. What an honor, and what an awesome responsibility! May you never take it lightly.

To the Mentor

If you have been selected to serve as a mentor for a new teacher, you should be honored. Someone, somewhere, has recognized your successes in the classroom and your leadership qualities. And, hopefully, you have been well trained in the art of mentoring. If not, please insist on it! No matter how good your teaching skills may be, mentoring is different from teaching, and it requires structured training.

As a mentor, you will play the role of teacher, friend, guide, coach, and role model. You will be expected to provide support, encouragement, a listening ear, a welcoming shoulder, constructive feedback, and suggestions for improvement. You will be required to exhibit professionalism, the ability to plan and organize, a love of children and teaching, excellence in teaching, good communication skills, good coaching skills, good conferencing skills, and an optimistic attitude. You will be responsible for maintaining confidentiality, sharing knowledge, skills and information with the new teacher, meeting frequently with the new teacher, observing the new teacher, providing demonstration lessons for the new teacher, familiarizing the new teacher with school policies, procedures, and culture, and participating in ongoing professional improvement activities. And, above all, you must be understanding, supportive, trustworthy, empathetic, innovative, knowledgeable, open-minded, reform-minded, and committed.

Does this sound a little overwhelming? Well, rest assured that your efforts will be rewarded a hundred-fold, because you will be positively affecting the lives of the new teachers you mentor, which will have a direct impact on every student that will ever enter their classroom doors.

Congratulations on being selected to mentor a new teacher, and thank you for accepting the challenge.

Common New-Teacher Challenges

Though all new teachers face a variety of challenges in the classroom, there are several that seem common to most. In fact, these are the same challenges that remain common for many seasoned teachers throughout their careers. These challenges include dealing with the overall management of the classroom, effectively handling discipline problems, dealing with difficult students, dealing with difficult coworkers, planning effectively, managing time wisely, remaining calm and professional in the face of unnerving situations, utilizing the most effective teaching strategies, accommodating individual differences in students, engaging students in critical thinking, etc.

This book is specifically designed to assist teachers in dealing with such challenges effectively. It is not loaded with fads, trends, educational jargon of the day, or the latest of educational innovations. Rather, it provides tried and true suggestions and techniques that will work for anyone willing to implement them. Quite simply, this book will truly help to enhance both teaching and learning. The opportunity to be the most effective teacher you can be awaits you, and the fact that you are reading this book says that you are seizing the opportunity and welcoming the challenge.

How to Use This Book

This book can be used in one of several ways. It is designed primarily to facilitate discussion between the mentor and the new teacher and to provide ideas and promote effective teaching on both the parts of the mentor and the new teacher. Of course, the ideas and teaching tips are universal and thus can be used by any teacher seeking to be more effective. All of the suggestions are easy to implement and will prove beneficial to both teachers and students. The 101 tips are divided into the following subheadings: *Classroom Management; Planning; Instruction; Professionalism: Attitudes and Behaviors of Effective Teachers; Motivation and Rapport;* and *A Teacher's Influence.* Therefore, if a new teacher is working on establishing effective classroom management, use the suggestions found under that section. By the same token, if a mentor needs to "brush up" on management skills to serve as a role model for the new teacher, the tips found there will be more than beneficial. Feel free to pick and choose any and all that seem appropriate for your classroom. However, use all of them if you want to truly enhance your effectiveness, whether you are a mentor, a first-time teacher, or any teacher seeking to better your skills.

The very fact that you are reading this says that you are a dedicated teacher who chooses to make a difference in the lives of the students you teach. This book will help to pave the way.

Classroom
Management

"You never get a second chance to make a first impression."

Source Unknown

Off to a Positive Start

We all know how important "first impressions" are. And the tone you set on the very first day of school will help to set the stage for the rest of the school year. Often, teachers dive straight into "teaching the content" from day one. This is a mistake. It is of the utmost importance that you let the students know who you are, that you give them the opportunity to begin to let you know who they are as individuals, and that you immediately "set them up for success." If you are a new teacher involved in an induction training process, you should already know exactly how your first day should be structured. If not, go to your mentor teacher for first-day instruction or find several successful veteran teachers and get a detailed account of what they do on the very first day of school. Rest assured that the most successful teachers begin, immediately, with structured procedures from day one. (See Tip 4 for more on procedures.)

Here are a few "musts" for starting off on a positive note:

- Greet your students at the door and welcome them.
- Be organized and well prepared. Plan every minute of your first day beforehand. (Structure is the key!)
- Have some type of clearly marked seating chart to avoid confusion as to where students should sit.
- Have some type of interesting assignment waiting for them so that they can get busy immediately upon entering the classroom—maybe an interest inventory.
- Remain calm, pleasant, and positive.
- Tell them what your expectations of them are and what they can expect from you and your class.
- Share with them your enthusiasm for teaching and your excitement about having each of them in your class.
- Express your belief that all of them will be successful.

> "The number one problem in the classroom is not discipline. It is the lack of procedures and routines."

Harry and Rosemary Wong

Classroom Management

If you were to ask your students who ride to school on a school bus, "How many of you noticed, really noticed, the tires on the bus this morning?" most, if not all, would say that they paid no attention to the tires. If you were then to ask, "How many of you think you might have noticed, when you got onto the bus this morning, if the tires had been missing?" most, if not all, would say that they would have taken definite notice because the bus would not have been able to transport them without its tires. Now take this scenario and relate it to classroom management. Classroom management is like the tires on the bus. If management is in place and the classroom runs smoothly, no one pays much attention to the management itself (except the teacher, of course, who has put much thought and effort into the classroom management plan). But if classroom management is missing, it's the same as having no tires on the bus. You notice it immediately. Just as the bus cannot run without tires, the classroom cannot run without management. Until the tires are on the bus, no children will be transported to school. Until classroom management is established, no learning can take place.

You see, contrary to popular belief, discipline is not the number one problem in the classroom. The lack of structured, well-rehearsed procedures and routines is what causes most discipline problems. Classroom management involves all that you do as a teacher to make your classroom run smoothly. Successful teachers know this. From the very first day of school, their routines and procedures are clear, and their students know what is expected of them. If you want to experience little or no discipline problems with your students, do not reinvent the wheel. Implement the basic tried and true management techniques of the most successful teachers. For the most practical, user-friendly, common sense approach to classroom management, purchase a copy of the book *The First Days of School* by Harry and Rosemary Wong.*

---

* Wong, H. K., & Wong, R. T. (1998). *The first days of school: How to be an effective teacher*. Mountain View, CA: Harry K. Wong Publications.

> "When designing an automobile, entertain infinite possibilities for the way of doing things. Once the design has hit the assembly line, allow for only one."

Annette L. Breaux

Have Procedures for Almost Everything

Some activities lend themselves to creative expression. Others do not. *Designing* an automobile lends itself to creative expression. *Assembling* the automobile does not. The same is true for classroom management. In order to successfully manage a classroom of students or any group of people, clearly defined procedures—consistent ways of doing things—must be established. Take 30 students and do not tell them how you want a thing done. They will each make up numerous ways to do the thing. Many of these ways will be unacceptable. You see, 30 students doing things their own way for even one task will allow for endless possibilities of how the task will be accomplished. This is good when teaching them how to think, but not so good when teaching them how to behave. So what kinds of activities require procedures in the classroom? Any activity that does not lend itself to creative expression requires procedures. For instance, you would not want your students "creating" ways of entering your classroom, or sharpening their pencils, or turning in assignments, or moving into groups, or walking to the lunchroom. As the person in charge of managing a group of students, it is your responsibility to establish procedures in order to ensure the smooth operation of your classroom environment. Tell your students what you expect, show them how you expect things to be done, practice the procedures with them, and reinforce as necessary.

Regarding learning and creating, set them free. Regarding behavior, show them the way.

"Discipline, like surgery, requires precision—no random cuts, no random comments. Above all, a teacher demonstrates self-discipline and good manners."

Haim Ginott

Discipline

The terms "discipline" and "classroom management" are often mistakenly used synonymously. Discipline is only one part of classroom management, albeit a vital one. Your discipline plan—and you must have one—consists of a set of a few rules. If a student breaks a rule, there must be a definite consequence. This consequence is not contingent upon the frustration level of the teacher at the time the rule was broken, but rather is predetermined as the plan is being devised.

Rules are devised to set limits, to help maintain order, and to protect people. On our public highways, there are speed limits. If the limit is exceeded, there is a consequence—a speeding ticket. This consequence is predetermined. Motorists are well aware of the consequence of exceeding the speed limit, just as students should be well aware of the consequences of breaking rules in your classroom. Therefore, devise a discipline plan and enforce it consistently.

In developing your plan, notice what the most effective teachers are doing to maintain structure and order in their classrooms. The real key to their success does not lie in the way that they discipline their students after the rules have been broken. Rather, they have established ways of preventing most, if not all, behavior problems through the structure of their classroom management plans along with their pleasant demeanors and proactive approaches to dealing with students. The simple fact is that in a well-managed environment, there are very few discipline problems!

"I teach eighth-grade alternative students in a high-poverty school where there are lots of troubled students. I've used the "Are You All Right?" technique for years and have yet to see it not work. I love it!"

Liz Breaux, Eighth-Grade Teacher,
Teacher of the Year, 2002

Use the "Are You All Right?" Technique

The "Are You All Right?" technique is based on the simple premise that children who believe you care about them are much more apt to behave. It works like this: If a student is doing something that is not appropriate during class, such as picking on others, talking excessively, refusing to do work, etc., simply step out into the hall with him/her and ask, "Are you all right?" with a sincere look of concern—not aggravation—on your face. Usually the student will answer "Yes," with a look of disbelief. You then say, "Well, the reason I'm asking is because the way you were behaving was inappropriate and so unlike you." (Okay, so you're stretching the truth a little, because the way he was acting may have been quite typical….) And then you say, "I knew that something must be bothering you for you to be acting that way, so I just wanted to know if you were all right and to let you know that if anything is bothering you, I'm here for you if you need to talk." That's it. You simply walk back into the classroom and resume teaching. And guess what happens? The student stops the misbehavior. And now you've accomplished several things—you've made the point that the behavior was inappropriate, you've maintained the student's dignity, you've acted out of concern instead of frustration, and you've let the student know that you care about him. What more could you want to accomplish?

> "I greet my students at the door every single day with a hug. I believe in making them feel welcomed, wanted, and special. Sadly, I know that for some students, it's the only hug they receive all day. I also know that when students feel welcomed in a classroom, they're much less likely to cause discipline problems. So it's a win-win situation."
>
> Rebecca Morrell,
> First-Grade Teacher

Greet Students Daily

If you walk into Walmart, you will be greeted by someone you very likely do not know. This person's job is to welcome every customer who walks into the store. When you walk into a department store, you will be greeted by a sales clerk who will be happy to assist you. When you walk onto an airplane, you are greeted and welcomed. When you go to a restaurant, you are greeted, seated, and waited upon. Why do these businesses spend so much money, time, and thought in assuring that their patrons feel welcomed upon entering their places of business? The reason is that people appreciate and respond to environments where they are made to feel welcomed and special. The same holds true for the classroom. All too often, teachers are busy making last minute preparations for class and thus do not stand at the door smiling and welcoming students as they enter. Not greeting your students every day may be one of the biggest mistakes you could ever make. Students who are welcomed as they enter the class are much more likely to "buy" what you are "selling." A simple smile and a genuine welcome will set the stage, every day, for a positive experience with your students. Just a handshake and a personal greeting offered to each student every day will help to earn the trust and respect of your students. Students like to be where they feel welcomed, and students succeed in positive environments. Happy, successful students? Any teacher will say "hello" to that!

> **"The art of being wise is knowing what to overlook."**
>
> William James

Learn What to Overlook

Children are not perfect, and neither are we. Teachers who expect perfect behavior from their students are being extremely unrealistic and are inviting profound disappointment. For example, if you are expecting that your students will never whisper to one another, you've lost touch with reality. And if the occasional "whispering" is not overly distracting, then overlook it. It's not a big deal. However, when many students begin talking and are off task, this should not be overlooked. The fact is that children will talk. They will make mistakes. They will act inappropriately at times. Why? Because they are children. Wise teachers know that if we get "nitpicky" about every little imperfection, we will literally run around putting out fires all day long, leaving little, if any, time for teaching. There is no "cookbook recipe" listing exactly what can and cannot be overlooked in the classroom, but the following should do the trick: Take a cup of common sense and mix with heaping spoonfuls of patience, understanding, consistency, positive expectations, and an enthusiastic attitude. Pour in a heart full of love, and bake for one school year.

Tip 7

> **"Reprove a friend in secret, but praise him before others."**

> Leonardo da Vinci

Handle Discipline Problems Discreetly

I call it the "faculty meeting rule," and it goes like this: Do not say or do anything to your students in the classroom that you would not feel comfortable having said or done to you in a faculty meeting. This is a good gauge, because just as teachers are among their peers in a faculty meeting and would not appreciate being singled out and embarrassed in front of their peers, students are among their peers in the classroom, and the same holds true for them. How would you feel if your principal singled you out and reprimanded you publicly for speaking during a faculty meeting? Most teachers would be mortified! Or, how would you feel if the principal announced the results of each teacher's observations in the midst of everyone else? These are issues that should be discussed privately. As teachers, we each have our own private "office." It's located right outside the classroom door, away from the rest of the students. Though it is not always possible to deal with every discipline challenge in total privacy, teachers can always use discretion. Discretion sometimes simply involves talking to a student at his desk in a quiet tone. Public reprimand simply does not work. It actually breeds resentment in students. Students will appreciate being treated with respect in such a situation and will recognize that you value their privacy. They are much more likely to correct the misbehavior when their dignity has been maintained. Also, students are not nearly as "tough" when you deal with them one-on-one, away from the audience of their classmates.

Tip 8

"Classroom management is the key to good teaching. When a teacher implements structured routines and procedures and teaches to the child's appropriate cognitive level, learning style, and interest level, discipline problems cease. Many times, teachers send 'discipline' problems to the principal's office, and the child is not the true problem! The problem stems from a lack of management. Also, referring students to the principal for minor infractions sends a message to the students that the teacher is not in control of the classroom. Effective teachers know this, and they handle their own discipline problems whenever possible, which is probably 99 percent of the time."

Cindy Eliser, Principal,
Louisiana's National Distinguished Principal, 2002

Handle Your Own Discipline Problems

It is often said that 90 percent of a school's discipline referrals come from 10 percent of the teachers. Can it be that the 10 percent have all of the "problem" students? Not likely. What is more probable is that the remaining 90 percent of the teachers are handling their own discipline problems. They know that students respect teachers who are both capable of, and willing to, maintain a positive, active, and safe learning environment. They know that students respect teachers who are in control. (Not "controlling," but rather "in" control.) This is not to say that effective teachers never have to refer student discipline problems to the office, but these incidences are rare and are thus taken seriously by both the administrator and the students. Common misbehaviors such as talking, inattentiveness, attention seeking, and teasing should be handled by the teacher.

A Little Praise

I helped a girl at school one day who had fallen and scraped her knee
I only did what any kid would've done if they were me
Then the teacher said that I was one of the nicest kids she'd met
And I thought to myself,"Well that's because she doesn't know me yet."
'Cause I'm really not so nice sometimes — I say and do bad things
I don't always finish my homework or come in right when the bell rings
But my teacher keeps on thinking that I'm really extra nice
So whenever I'm around her, I'm nice, not once, but twice
I even work much harder when I am in her class
Instead of going really slow, I finish extra fast
She always takes the time to notice everything good that I do
She's told me I'm special so many times that I think it's becoming true.

Annette L. Breaux,
No Adults Allowed

"Catch" Students Behaving

As teachers, we are trained to recognize problems, diagnose the causes of the problems, and then respond accordingly to solve these problems. That's a fact, and it is a necessary skill that any good teacher must possess. But how many of us were ever trained to recognize good behavior, diagnose what's causing the good behavior, and then foster the behavior so that it will continue? Not many. Think about it: We all have "eyes in the backs of our heads" and can spot a child misbehaving from a mile away! Again, this is a good skill to possess. But an even more important skill is to be able to use those same "eyes in the backs of our heads" to spot a child behaving well and encourage that good behavior or kind deed. A simple "Thanks for raising your hand" or "I really appreciate the cooperation I'm observing with this group" can work wonders. Students crave our attention, and they will usually do whatever it takes to get it. When they learn that they are much more apt to get your attention by behaving, they begin behaving. Teachers who focus on good behavior more so than misbehavior have far fewer discipline problems in their classrooms. So be on the lookout for good behavior. You'll begin to notice it everywhere!

"One of the tests of leadership is the ability to recognize a problem before it becomes an emergency."

Arnold H. Glasow

Be Proactive

When students begin to get bored, what does it look like? When a child is upset, what does it look like? When children are "thinking" about misbehaving, what does it look like? Anyone who has ever been around children or who has ever "been" a child, which should cover most of us, can easily answer all of these questions. And anyone who can answer these questions can be proactive. Being "proactive" simply means recognizing *potential* problems and stopping them before they become *actual* problems. Here is an example that epitomizes a teacher using a proactive approach to problem solving—or rather, problem preventing. I went to the door of a classroom one day to speak with a teacher. As we were speaking, she noticed that Tremain was out of his desk, heading toward Jonathan to hit him. The teacher immediately looked at him and said, "Tremain, thank you so much for going over to help Jonathan. I was just bragging to Ms. Breaux about how helpful you all are in this class, and there you are demonstrating it. Thank you, Tremain. I really appreciate your thoughtfulness." Tremain, totally caught off guard and completely distracted from his original "mission," walked on over to Jonathan and helped him with his work. This, of course, was how the teacher handled every potential problem. She recognized it and immediately "broke the pattern" of the student. She turned the potentially negative situation around and always managed to make it a positive one. If students were appearing bored, she changed the activity. When a child walked into class looking upset, she spoke to the child privately, listened, and expressed concern. When a child was contemplating an inappropriate behavior, she often asked the child a question, completely unrelated to what was about to happen, in order to defuse the potential problem. It worked for this teacher, and it will work for you. Oh, and speaking of working, children work much harder and behave much better in the classrooms of proactive teachers.

*Have you ever noticed how much pent up energy
students have as they burst out of the schoolhouse
doors at the end of the day?*

Provide Frequent Stretch Breaks

I've often heard teachers complain about having to sit in meetings for "over an hour," or better yet, having to endure an all-day training session, fighting to stay awake throughout. I've also witnessed how much talking goes on between the participants—off-task behavior, of course—during many of these meetings. Why is this? Basically, it's because teachers are active people. They are accustomed to moving around, "doing" things, and rarely sitting still during the day. The teachers walk out of the school building at the end of the day looking exhausted because they've been working all day long. So why is it that the students look so energetic? Could it be because they've been inactive for too long? Could it be that they've been literally sitting down most of the day? And is it possible that students tend to get off task or talk at inappropriate times because they are restless and in desperate need of some action? Shouldn't the students be the ones who look exhausted at the end of the day? Absolutely. So how can this be accomplished? First, we, as teachers, need to become aware of the amount of time that our students are expected to remain seated during our classes. Students *need* to be kept so busy that they don't have time to misbehave or become off-task. This is not to say that the desks should be removed from the classrooms. Many classroom activities require students to be seated in their desks. But teachers who are "aware" of the energy just waiting to come out of those young bodies and minds use that awareness to their advantage. Here's how it's done: When you notice that students have been seated for more than thirty minutes or so (or even less for younger students), provide a stretch break. I recently observed a teacher who, out of nowhere, it appeared, would say to the class, "Okay, when I say 'go,' you will have 45 seconds to stand up, stretch, and talk to your neighbors. Remember, however, that when I say 'stop,' you must be seated and quiet immediately. During a one-hour lesson, he did this three times. The students followed the procedure beautifully, and it appeared that they were accustomed to doing this. I also noted that the teaching activities moved quickly, the pace was steady, and the students remained on task throughout the lesson. Following the lesson, I asked the teacher about the frequent breaks. He smiled and said, "Oh, that. I don't know about you, but I know that I can't manage to sit still for more than twenty minutes at a time, and I'm much older than my students, so I don't have near the energy that they do. I make it a practice to provide frequent stretch breaks. As you probably noticed, the breaks don't last long, but they work! I've also noticed that students are able to maintain more of a focus if they are allowed to stand up, stretch, talk a little, and keep their blood flowing. It literally re-energizes them, and I need for my students to focus all the energy they have on what we're learning." He went on to explain that even during times of active student participation involving group work, he still took time to give the students stretch breaks so that they could re-energize and refocus. "My students work hard in here," he said. "I want them to leave my classroom enlightened, inspired, and a little exhausted every day. If they don't, then I'm not doing my job."

> "In dealing with students, I have found that I rarely have to verbally acknowledge misbehaviors. Rather, I simply use 'proximity' and move closer to the student who is off task. Standing next to a student is an effective, nonthreatening way of defusing the problem. I make it a point to move around the classroom a lot as I teach so that it does not seem strange when I stand next to a particular student's desk."
>
> Jeni Russell,
> Mentor/Teacher

Use Proximity

"Have you ever noticed that the 'problem' students always gravitate to the back of the classroom?" asked a teacher during a pre-observation conference. "It never fails," he said. "My behavior problems, every year, come from the back of the room." Upon observing this teacher, I noted that he never ventured past the front row of desks in the classroom. And what do you know? The further back the students sat, the more they talked! Seated in the back of the room myself, I was almost tempted to join in the conversation, as I felt completely removed from both the teacher and the lesson. All the action was in the front of the room, so the students in the back chose to create their own action. I also noted that the only time the students in the back were acknowledged was with verbal reprimands or the "teacher eye" when the noise escalated. After the lesson, I asked the teacher if he would be willing to attempt an experiment in order to possibly alleviate the difficulties he was experiencing with the "problem" students. He readily agreed to participate. The experiment involved his use of proximity. For one week, I asked him to spend his teaching time moving around the classroom, spending time among the students as opposed to staying in front of the class. He also agreed that when a student was talking or was off task, he would calmly move closer to that student without the use of the "teacher eye" or verbal reprimands. One week later, I sat in the same classroom, but it definitely did not "feel" like the same classroom. Amazingly, the "problem" students had become actively involved in the lessons. Instead of talking to one another, they were now involved in discussions with the teacher. And, not to my surprise, the teacher was noticeably more enthusiastic in his delivery. "I can't believe it," he said to me after the lesson. "How could I have missed that? I've been blaming the students for the five years I've been teaching. And the answer was so simple. I'm actually enjoying teaching now, and I can tell that the students are enjoying my lessons more." The simple fact is that physical distance equals mental distance in the classroom. So get in there with your students. Consider yourself a "coach" in the middle of the huddle. Your team is sure to score lots of touchdowns!

Do not ask a question unless you are prepared to receive an answer....

Do Not Provoke Defensiveness

The following are actual teacher questions and the resulting student answers:

Teacher: How many times do I have to tell you?
Student: 6,284.

Teacher: Don't you have any home training?
Student: My daddy is in jail, and my mother is on crack!

Teacher: Do you want me to send you to the office?
Student: Actually, yes. It would be a pleasant diversion.

Teacher: Do you have a problem?
Student: No, but you do!

Teacher: Don't you know this material?
Student: If I did, then I guess you'd be out of a job!

In all of the above scenarios, can you guess at what the teachers' reactions were? You guessed it. The teachers were horrified and highly insulted. Though I am not, in any way, suggesting that the students' answers were the most appropriate ones, I am suggesting that these teachers "set themselves up" for the answers they received. These teachers were acting, as we often tend to do, out of anger and frustration. In actuality, they were fueling the exact behaviors they were trying to diminish. The simple fact is that sarcastic questions provoke sarcastic answers. And, as we discuss in Tip 85, there is no place for sarcasm in the classroom. If a student is struggling, instead of asking, "Do you have a problem?" in a sarcastic tone, simply say, "I notice that you're struggling with this, and I'd like to help." Then do just that—assist the student. In the last question and answer above, the student actually made a very valid point—if students knew all the answers and exhibited perfect behavior and ample amounts of self-motivation, we would all be out of jobs!

Tip 14

FACT: If you give a student nothing to do, he'll find something to do, and it usually won't be what you had in mind!

Avoid "Down" Time

To begin with, let's define "down" time. "Down" time consists of any time that a student has nothing to do. When does "down" time typically occur in the classroom? It usually occurs when students finish an assignment early, when the teacher finishes a lesson before the end of the class period, or during transitions from one subject to the next. That's the problem. Here's the solution: Simply put, the way to avoid "down" time is to structure every minute of the entire class period. In other words, when giving an assignment, provide structured activities for early finishers. A note of caution here: Just because a student finishes early does not mean that he has completed the assignment correctly. Determine that first, and then you will know whether to provide enrichment activities or remediation activities at that point. Regardless, the student will keep busy. Next, do not make the mistake of under-planning where you may have several minutes at the end of the period during which students have nothing to do. As stated above, when students have nothing to do, they'll find something to do, and it usually won't be to your liking! Teach from "bell to bell." Regarding transitions, implement structured procedures that make the transitions smooth and efficient. My favorite example comes from my own classroom experiences. I noted that during transitions, where I would instruct the students to put one set of materials away and prepare for the next subject, it was inevitable that the following would occur: Some students would be ready to go in seconds, some were seated on the floor looking inside of their desks, some would start cleaning out the insides of their desks, some would engage in conversations with others, etc. And these transitions were eating away at valuable teaching and learning time. So I began to do the following, which has continued to work wonders for me and for many others with whom I have shared the technique—at all age levels, I might add. I discovered that students enjoy being "timed" during transitions, and I used that discovery to implement a procedure. I would say, "Okay, don't move until I say 'go.' But when I say 'go,' I want for you to pick up your reading books and get out your language projects from yesterday. I'm going to be timing you, and the Guinness Book of World Records for seventh graders is 9.243 seconds. (Of course, I was just fabricating this!) When you're ready to go, give me a 'thumbs up.' And when all thumbs are up, I'll record your time. Go!" Amazingly, it worked! Within seconds, all students were ready to go and anxious to see if they had set the new world record.

Even more amazingly, I would hit my watch when I said 'go' and hit it again when all thumbs were up. Then I would say something like, "Wow! You did that in 8.987 seconds. You've got the new world record!" I was just wearing a plain old watch—not a stopwatch—and the students never figured that out! They even began competing with my other classes to see if they could beat one another's times. Oh, and they never tired of it! So give it a try. It's great fun, students love the idea, it adds excitement, and it saves time and aggravation. The record set by my class was 5.3245678932 seconds. I challenge you to beat that!

> **"We must have ... a place where children can have a whole group of adults they can trust."**
>
> Margaret Mead

Put Students at Ease

Research has shown, time and again, that when we are feeling anxious or nervous, our brains begin to focus solely on ways to relieve the anxiety. Research also shows that our brains take much longer to process a negative statement than to process a positive statement. You know what? We didn't even need the research to tell us that. Just think about it. When you're upset about something, it becomes your focus because you want to feel better. Not exactly rocket science! Now consider this one: When someone pays you a compliment, you generally thank the person and move on. It feels nice to receive a compliment, but the compliment doesn't overtake your thinking. On the other side of that, if someone insults you or upsets you by saying something negative to you or about you, you feel upset, and then you begin trying to figure out why the person said what was said. You may even begin to experience a little righteous indignation. You usually get angry, and that anger sometimes leads to retaliation. But the fact is that no matter how hard you try to let it go, your brain wants to focus on it for a while. It's a lot tougher to just "move on" when someone says something negative about you than it is when someone says something positive about you.

Okay, so what are the ramifications of this in the classroom? Again, it doesn't take a rocket scientist to understand that in a negative environment—one where students are fearful, uncomfortable, and anxious—very little learning can take place because all of those young brains are too busy focusing on trying to feel LESS fearful, LESS uncomfortable, and LESS anxious. You, as a teacher, can "nip this one in the bud" very easily and very early on. Here's how to do it: On the very first day of school, make it your number one priority to put your students at ease. Display a calm, composed demeanor. Make everything about you and your classroom say, "Welcome! I'm glad you're here." And then do one of the most important things you will do all year: Make promises to your students. Begin, when you introduce yourself, NOT by telling them what you expect of them, but what *they* can expect of *you*. Tell them about how exciting your class will be. Then make the following two promises to them:

1. I will never raise my voice in this classroom. That's right. I will not yell at you. That is not to say that I won't deal with misbehav-

ior and hold you accountable, because I will. But I promise that I will deal with you in a private manner and treat each one of you with respect. (Oh, and you don't have to add, "And I'll expect you to treat me with respect also," because students will automatically treat you with respect once they know you respect them!)

2. I will never "put you on the spot" or try to embarrass you in front of your peers. So relax. You're safe here, and you're going to be amazed at how much we're all going to learn this year!

By making these two promises, you have accomplished two things:

1. You have just made yourself accountable to your students. Who better to hold you accountable? In case you don't yet know this, students will "hold you to your promises." And you'll lose their trust if you ever break a promise. So, basically, you've just taken the option of "losing your cool" away from yourself!

2. You have managed to put your students "at ease." And when students are at ease, they will do their best, they will accept challenges, they will behave, they will succeed, and most importantly, they will never forget you for it!

"Your very first priority when students enter your classroom is to get them working."

Harry K. Wong

Provide Structured "Bellwork"

Why is it that some classrooms seem chaotic the second the students enter? And why is it that, in other classrooms, students enter and begin to work immediately? The answer is very simple. Effective teachers know that they must have structured bellwork awaiting the students each day as they enter the classroom. What is bellwork? Bellwork is an assignment that is posted in the same place every day for students to begin as soon as they walk into the room. The assignment is brief and interesting to the students, and it relates to the lesson that will be taught that day. Let's say that you will be discussing our country's justice system for the day's lesson. For the daily bellwork, you might have the following assignment posted:

> Pretend that as of today, there are no more school rules. All students are free to do what they wish, with no limitations. Think about this for a minute, and then write three examples of realistic situations that could occur as a result of having no rules. Then, list three reasons you believe that rules are/are not necessary in this school.

This bellwork assignment would take only a few minutes and would lead into a discussion of societal rules, laws, consequences, etc.

One of the keys to successful classroom management is to keep students actively involved from the moment they walk in until the moment they leave. Busy students are successful students, and busy students are behaving students, as they have no time for anything else. So keep them busy, keep them on task, wear them out, and enjoy your sanity!

Tip 17

If I Could

If I could then I would
Whether or not you think I should
I wouldn't because I couldn't
Not because you think I shouldn't
But I can't so I won't
And since I won't then I don't
Now should you feel confused
Or should you feel amused?
Since you won't tell me what I should
Then I won't tell you, but I could.

Annette L. Breaux,
No Adults Allowed

Avoid Power Struggles with Students

So often, teachers relinquish control by engaging in meaningless power struggles with students. I was recently observing in a teacher's seventh-grade classroom when one of the students strutted in and announced to the class, "Guess what? My daddy won the lottery last night, and he said I could quit school. So good riddance to all of you!" I have to admit that I was amazed when the teacher simply looked at him, smiled, and said, "Boy, aren't you lucky!" and she immediately began teaching. The student had no comeback because he, too, was amazed and, I suppose, a little shocked. He simply went to his seat. I am quite sure that the student was attempting to provoke a struggle. However, it takes two people, and one wasn't playing. The teacher did not react, nor did she attack. And the story doesn't end there. The teacher later shared with me that the student stayed after class and apologized for his outburst. He said, "I'm sorry about the way I came into class. And I was just kidding about my daddy winning the lottery."

Now consider the same scenario in the classroom of a teacher who is willing to engage in power struggles with students. It probably would have gone something like this:

Student: " Guess what? My daddy won the lottery last night, and he said I could quit school. So good riddance to all of you!"

Teacher: "First of all, young man, your daddy did not win the lottery because we would have heard about it by now. Secondly, you're not old enough to quit school. And lastly, don't you ever come barging into my classroom again insulting your fellow class-mates and me like that!"

Can you imagine where this could lead?

Again, effective teachers do not engage in power struggles with students. They defuse the situation immediately by not providing the student with the desired response, and they maintain their composure. Quite simply, they do not add fuel to the fire.

FACT: Logical consequences breed logical results!
Illogical consequences breed illogical results!

Make the Punishment Fit the Misbehavior

I once watched a teacher punish a student who was talking out of turn. The punishment consisted of writing the entire text that he was supposed to be reading at the time of the misbehavior. I then thought to myself, "Wait a minute. This is a language arts teacher. Isn't she supposed to be instilling a love of reading and writing in these students? And isn't this punishment making the act of writing seem tedious and boring? Is she not turning this student off, fostering the same behavior for which she's punishing him?" There was no logic to this punishment. Following the lesson, I asked her about her choice of punishment and her desired result. She answered, "Well, I wanted for him to pay attention and to stop talking out of turn." "Did it work?" I asked. "No, not at all. He became quite defensive and refused to do the work. He threw his pencil aside and said he couldn't write all of that. Then he began talking again." "Why did you choose this particular punishment?" I asked. "I didn't know what else to do. His talking was aggravating me, so I just said the first thing that came to my mind." My suggestion to her was to try to make the punishment fit the misbehavior next time. She decided that a logical response to the misbehavior might be have been to talk to him privately and let him know that his behavior was inappropriate and distracting to the other students. Then, as a consequence, he would not be allowed to talk during the break between subjects, in which students were allowed one minute of talking and stretching time.

The above scenario is a common one. Teachers get frustrated, and they say things like, "If you don't stop it, you'll never see another recess." Or better yet, they make students write something like, "I will not talk out of turn" several hundred times. Where's the logic in that? There is none. Can you imagine being pulled over by a policeman who has had a frustrating day and decides to take your car away for a year as a punishment for having a broken headlight? Or can you imagine being caught doing what all teachers do—talking during a faculty meeting—and having to write, "I will not talk during faculty meetings" 500 times? These consequences are not logical, and they would only breed resentment. You do not want to breed resentment in students. Rather, you want to instill in them that rules are rules and they exist for a reason. If they choose to break a rule, then a logical consequence will follow. Remember: Make the punishment match the misbehavior, not your current level of frustration.

> **"An eye for an eye makes the whole world blind."**
>
> Mahatma Gandhi

Attack the Problem, Not the Person

One of the biggest mistakes a teacher can make is to confuse the problem with the person. The two must be separated in order to truly deal with any problem or any person effectively. Let's make the concept simple. A student is consistently failing tests. You, as a teacher, know that this student is quite capable. Attacking the person would sound like this: "Look, young lady, I know you're capable, and I want you to start putting forth some effort and paying attention in class. You should be making A's, and instead you're making F's. What's the matter with you?" Notice the sarcasm in the teacher's words and the blame placed upon the person. Also notice that the teacher, unaware of the cause of the problem, poses a "solution" for the student. Now let's consider the same scenario where the teacher attacks the problem instead of the person: "Rebecca, I notice that you're struggling with your grades. Knowing how capable you are, I'm concerned and was wondering if you could shed some light on what's going on. You seem to be distracted from your studies. Maybe I can help." Do you hear the difference in the approach? Do you see how, in this scenario, the student's dignity is maintained as the focus is on the problem and not the person? It is human nature to defend against personal attack, and students are definitely human.

One teacher summarized it quite well after I witnessed an interesting encounter she had with a student. The student walked into class very upset about something that had happened on the playground. She immediately began picking on another student in the classroom. The teacher asked her to be seated and the student retaliated with, "Leave me alone, you _____" (I'm sure you can fill in the expletive.) The teacher very calmly whispered something to the student, the student sat down, and the teacher began teaching, as if nothing had happened. After she got the class busy, she walked out with the student and had a private discussion. Following class, I said, "I was impressed with how calmly you handled that situation. I'm also curious as to what it was you said when you whispered to her and calmed her down." The teacher smiled and said, "Well, this student just moved here. So she doesn't know me well enough yet to determine whether I am a _____ or not. I may be, or I may not be, but she'll have to get to know me better before she can make such a statement. So I simply leaned over and explained what I just said to you. I told her that I would give her a few minutes to regain her composure and then we would deal with what had just happened. And of course, we did deal with it, and I learned a lot about that student in a little bit of time." I then asked, "Do you always handle such situations this calmly and professionally?" Once again, the teacher smiled and said, "I believe that if we, as teachers, really knew the faces behind the masks of some students, and if we understood what caused them to behave so inappropriately at times, and if we had any idea what struggles some of these students face, what cumbersome emotional loads some of them are carrying around, then 9 times out of 10, we would be heartbroken instead of angry." She followed that by saying, "Please understand that I don't excuse their behaviors. But my attitude and the beliefs that I just shared with you enable me to attack the problem instead of the person. I love those kids, and whether they accept that love or not, I keep loving them anyway. Sooner or later, they all come around when they realize that I do care and that I won't attack." "How soon do you think this particular student will come around?" I asked. "She already did," replied the teacher. "How can you be sure?" I asked. "I just know," she said. "And it's the best feeling in the world!"

Planning

> "I work with new teachers daily, and they all seem to struggle with time management—especially with regard to planning. It's so difficult for a new teacher to know how much time a particular lesson or activity will take, how and when to find the time outside of the school day to plan lessons and take care of paperwork, and how to schedule time to maintain some semblance of a life outside of teaching."
>
> Alyson Naquin,
> Curriculum Facilitator

Manage Your Time Wisely

A new teacher came into my office crying one day, saying, "I just can't do this. There aren't enough hours in the day." "Aren't enough hours in the day to do what?" I asked. "To be a teacher and still have a life—to grade papers, plan lessons, and do paperwork, still managing to take care of my family at home. It's just not possible. I think I've chosen the wrong profession. My family is also beginning to suffer, because all I do is schoolwork, and I can't allow that to continue." I asked her to map out her day for me—to tell me her typical routine. It went like this:

♦ Wake up, and either grade a paper or two or spend a few minutes planning.

♦ Make breakfast, and try to grade another paper or two while eating.

♦ Get ready for school and get my child ready.

♦ Arrive at school, sign in, get a little more work done—usually while visiting with coworkers.

♦ Teach all day—with one hour of planning time, usually spent listening to the gripes of other coworkers.

♦ Come home from school and spend all afternoon and evening trying to juggle cooking, cleaning, grading papers, planning lessons, doing homework with my child, etc.

♦ Cry myself to sleep in the wee hours of the morning!

Okay, I knew I had to help this teacher, who was an excellent new teacher, to develop some time-management skills. You see, what she was doing was running from one activity to the next, never really finishing one thing before she moved on to another. It would be overwhelming for any teacher, even an experienced one, to try to accomplish what she was trying to accomplish on such a schedule. So I made a simple suggestion that literally changed her life! I asked her how much focused time she had set aside every day to be completely alone with planning and paperwork. The answer, as you saw from her schedule, was none. I then asked if it would be possible to either come to school one hour earlier or stay one hour later—ALONE—in her classroom. She said that it would be possible to come one hour earlier, because her husband brought her child to school in the mornings. So we agreed that she would spend one hour, every morning, of uninterrupted planning time. We also "found" another hour during the day—her planning period. She agreed that instead of going into the teachers' lounge with her stack of paperwork, listening to and engaging in conversations with others, she would now spend that time in her room, alone.

The results? I received a phone call a little over a week later from the teacher. She said, "You saved my life! I'm sticking to my schedule, and it's working. I don't even have to take work home with me anymore. I have my life back, with plenty of time left over. And I'm managing to stay on top of my planning, grading, and paperwork."

"Oh," she added, "and both my students and my family have noticed that I'm a much nicer and happier person!"

> **"Effective teaching may be the hardest job there is."**
>
> William Glasser

Understand that Teaching Is Hard Work

There is an immense misconception floating around out there that "teachers have it made." After all, they only work seven hours a day, they have weekends free, they get lots of holidays, and they enjoy an extended summer vacation. What a breeze! Well, whoever sent that message afloat obviously was never a teacher. Teaching is quite possibly the most demanding of all professions. The good news is that it is, without doubt, the most rewarding and noble profession of all!

Regrettably, many new teachers enter the profession with no concept of what will be required of them. They are often shocked to learn of all the paperwork and planning time involved, all the skills that are required to teach and manage a classroom effectively, all the patience, understanding and empathy they must possess, all the many hats they must wear, all the problems some students bring to school with them, etc.

Please understand that teaching is hard work! The road will be rocky at times. You will stumble and fall on occasion. You may even bleed a little. But understand, also, that nothing worthwhile comes easily. The rewards of teaching far outweigh the demands. You will know this the first time you make a child smile, the first time you receive a sweaty hug, the first time you dry a student's tears on your shirt sleeve, the first time you open a present with crinkled wrapping paper and way too much tape, and any time you witness the slightest or greatest of achievements and the least or most concerted of efforts from the children whose very lives you are helping to shape.

Yes, teaching is hard work. And this noblest of professions is reserved only for those willing to rise to meet all of its many challenges, to give of themselves completely and then give some more, and to be humble enough to accept, with dignity and grace, its awesome responsibilities.

Tip 22

> "Never put off till tomorrow what you can do today."
>
> Lord Chesterfield

I'll Do It Tomorrow

I didn't feel like doing it, so I put it off for a day
And the next day came and I put off more—Too much was coming my way
I used up tons of paper with my list of "things to do"
And every day my "list of things" just grew and grew and grew
It overtook my kitchen, then overtook my house
It overtook my children and it overtook my spouse
If only I had done the things that needed to be done
It would have been much easier to do things one by one
But now I'm overwhelmed with all the things I did not do
How will I survive this? I do not have a clue!
And sitting atop these things to do are feelings of guilt and sorrow
So I'm turning over a new leaf. Yep, I'll do it tomorrow!

Annette L. Breaux

Do Not Procrastinate

Remember—

It's much better to be on top of your workload than to have your workload on top of you! Don't put it off one more minute. Take a step. Begin it!

> "I remember hearing Harry Wong hit the nail on the head when he said, 'If you're failing to plan, you're planning to fail.' We saw a drastic change in our teaching when we trained all of our teachers in the basic parts of an effective lesson—task focus, lesson presentation, guided practice, independent practice, and review. It became a district mandate that all teachers plan and teach this way, and it has had a tremendous impact on the effectiveness of teaching."
>
> Elmo Broussard, Superintendent

Plan Effective Lessons

Yes, if you're failing to plan, you're planning to fail. It's that simple. And don't ever think that your students will not know if you're "winging it." They see it, they sense it, and they respond to the lack of structure accordingly! The fact is that planning does take time, skill, and thought, but when you plan well, then most of your work is done. Now you can go and have fun teaching the lesson. Teachers who do not plan good lessons end up struggling with behavior problems, off- task students, and general chaos, not to mention that in order for the students to learn a new skill, the lesson must be well thought out and well taught. Good planning is a skill and it requires training, patience, practice, and guidance. Mentors can play a critical role in spending time planning with new teachers.

Remember, surgeons go into surgery with a highly structured plan, coaches go into games with a very specific game plan, and attorneys appear in court to defend their clients with very detailed plans. We would expect no less of them, and thus, in teaching our children, we should expect no less of ourselves.

Tip 24

"Good order is the foundation of all good things."

Edmond Burke

Be Organized and Prepared

Organization is not a skill that comes naturally or easily to some. However, it is a skill that *must* be acquired if you desire to be an effective teacher. First of all, an organized room gives the message that the teacher is competent and well prepared. And in organized environments, students tend to be more organized, more respectful of the classroom property, more respectful of the teacher, and better behaved. Students want and need structure. They want a teacher who is well prepared and well organized. Knowing where everything is—a place for everything, and everything in its place—makes for a calmer environment. I have often noticed that when classrooms are in disarray and the teacher is running from here to there trying to locate materials during the lesson or trying to fill in with something to keep the students busy because the lesson was not well prepared, the students tend to mimic that behavior. The bottom line is this: If your classroom is an ordered, highly functional place, the students will mimic that environment. And when teachers are organized and prepared, there is very little, if any, time for off-task behavior. The class runs very smoothly, from bell to bell. Procedures are established, materials are readily available, the room is not cluttered or dirty, the lessons flow very smoothly, and the whole environment is that of a safe, orderly, inviting place to learn.

Now let's look at the other side of that. I walked into a teacher's classroom some time back, and I couldn't believe my eyes. There was "stuff" everywhere. Student projects were lying around all over the floor, the desks just seemed to be scattered around, there were stacks and stacks of books and papers everywhere, the teacher's desk looked like it had been struck by a tornado, and there was even garbage that "hadn't quite made it" into the garbage can. The teacher was literally running between activities trying to find this worksheet or that lesson plan or some textbook—noticeably flustered. The students were out of their desks, talking, roaming about. One student actually tripped on one of many obstructions in the aisle. For one solid hour, I can say that I witnessed no actual teaching and learning. Everyone just sort of blended in with the mess. In one word, "chaos." The teacher apologized for the mess and jokingly said, "The custodian won't even come in here to clean." Needless to say, we saw to it that she received some guidance from her mentor and from a few other willing teachers who agreed to spend a Saturday helping her to get organized. Though things are not quite ordered yet, she has come a long way.

Imagine walking into a doctor's office where you come in on two legs and walk out on crutches due to tripping on some of the mess on the floor. Imagine going into a courtroom where the judge can't find his gavel, the jury is walking around and talking, there's paper strewn all over the floor, and the attorneys have to keep stopping so that they can run out to their cars to find some of their missing evidence. Would you feel like you're getting a fair shot in either of these scenarios? Well, students are not getting a fair shot in disorderly classroom environments.

Again, students need structured, ordered, welcoming environments. And it is important that they see their teacher as a true professional—one who is always prepared and who structures the class so that lessons flow, students are kept busy, and no one's life is at risk among the chaos!

"Accurate documentation (grade books, attendance records, behavior tracking, portfolios, notes to parents, etc.) is both important and necessary. It allows teachers to track student progress and provide valuable feedback to all concerned parties. It also promotes parents' involvement in the education of their children."

Sandy Holloway, Principal

Maintain Accurate Records

In this day and age, we hear so much about accountability and the importance of maintaining accurate and thorough records on each of our students. "What if a parent sues us because he refuses to believe that his child can do any wrong?" "With the new statewide testing of students, will I lose my job if my students don't score well?" "I witnessed the fight with my own two eyes, and I documented everything I saw—just in case there's a lawsuit." The list goes on and on. And though I am in no way implying that these are not real and important issues, I choose not to focus on these issues here. Rather, I choose to focus on the importance of maintaining accurate records for the sake of improving student achievement and providing parents and key educators involved in each child's education with the information they need to do just that—improve each child's education. I believe that the day that I begin tracking student progress and behavior out of "fear" is the day that I should leave the teaching profession.

So what benefits are there for students if a teacher maintains accurate records? The benefits are simple—improved teaching and learning! I was called in to a school recently to help deal with a "problem" child. The child had two teachers, only one of whom was having difficulties with him, so I decided to acquire input from both of them. When I spoke with the first teacher and asked her to tell me about Thomas, she responded, "Let me get my grade book and I'll show you his grades." In the grade book, next to Thomas's name, were all failing grades on all graded assignments. I then asked the teacher to tell me about Thomas's strengths. She responded, "He has no real strengths, as you can see from his grades." "What does he struggle with most?" I asked. "Everything," she responded. "He won't behave, and he refuses to put any effort into his schoolwork." I asked if she had work samples, behavior records, documentation of anything she was doing to improve the situation, etc. The only things she could produce were several test papers with big fat red "F's" on them—no comments, nothing. I then asked what types of unique approaches she was taking or strategies she was using to accommodate his specific needs. Once again, she could give me nothing. I thought to myself, "How can you accommodate a student's needs if you don't even know what his needs are?" There was no doubt in my mind as to why Thomas was "drowning" in this teacher's classroom.

I then moved on to the next teacher. Not only did she provide me with a grade book, but she presented a portfolio of Thomas's work, letters of communication with Thomas's father, a picture of Thomas from a bulletin board, a letter that Thomas had written to her, a chart on Thomas's behavior, samples of graded assignments on which she had written lots of comments (most of which were positive, and all of which were constructive), and last, but definitely not least, teacher notes that specified unique approaches and strategies she used to teach Thomas, with red asterisks next to those that were most successful. Needless to say, Thomas, though not making straight A's, posed no problems, academically or behaviorally, in this teacher's classroom. She went on to tell me, without my asking, about all of Thomas's strengths—his outgoing personality, his leadership qualities, his creativity, and his resolute determination to succeed, especially when things did not come easily to him. Was this the same Thomas? Yes it was, but I would have never known it by listening to the two "eye witness" accounts! The first teacher complained that it was impossible to get any support from Thomas's father. The second told me just the opposite. Same Thomas, same father, different teachers. You decide.

Bottom line: Effective teachers maintain accurate documentation in order to track student progress, to search for patterns in student learning and behavior, to adjust teaching accordingly, and to communicate effectively with parents. Needless to say, the lives of all the "Thomases" in their classrooms are profoundly affected by their influence.

FACT: If you know where you're going, you're much more likely to get there.

Make the Objectives "Clear" for Each Lesson

"What did you learn in school today?" ask many parents when their children return home. "I don't know," answer far too many children. "Well, what did you do?" ask the parents. "Well, we had to write a lot and read some stories and read a chapter and answer the questions at the end of the chapter and fill out a lot of stupid worksheets!" Okay, so now we know what they did, but we still don't know what they learned! Therefore, we must ask the question here, "Does a teacher who engages students in the aforementioned activities have clear objectives for each lesson—and does the teacher make those objectives known to the students?"

Imagine going on a vacation and having no destination. How would you know what to pack? Imagine a doctor performing surgery without an objective. "Oh well, I'll just open him up and take a look around and see what's what!" Or imagine being the patient, where you know you'll be undergoing surgery, but you have no idea why! I know it seems ridiculous. But it's just as ridiculous for students to be unclear on exactly what it is they're supposed to be accomplishing.

Simply stated, an objective defines what the students should know or be able to do at the end of each lesson. I've often watched teachers tell students to read a chapter and answer the questions at the end of the chapter when they're finished. The students reluctantly get busy, but they have no idea "why" they have to do this. In fact, it's a good rule to know that when students ask, "Why do we have to do this?" it's like a red flag reminding you that you have obviously forgotten to make the objective for the lesson clear. It goes without saying that you, the teacher, must write clear, measurable objectives for every lesson you teach. But that's not enough. You must now make those objectives clear to your students. Make it a point, as you begin each lesson, to tell your students, "Guess what you'll be able to do at the end of this lesson," and then tell them. That way, you'll know where you're going, students will know what they're learning, and you'll all arrive home from your vacation safely with no unexplainable surgical scars!

Isn't it true that most students experience a complete personality change when a substitute teacher walks into the classroom?

Provide a Plan for Substitutes

I remember it like yesterday. It was my first year of teaching, and I had to attend a meeting. It was going to be the first day of school that I had ever missed. Still wearing my rose-colored glasses and never having left my seventh graders in the hands of a substitute teacher, I never anticipated what "could" and probably "would" happen during my absence. I thought I had all of my bases covered. I had left explicit instructions for the substitute teacher—down to the last detail. I told my students I would be out, that a substitute teacher would be with them, and that I would see them the day after. By this time, I had my classroom management system well organized. My students knew what I expected, and they followed all of my procedures beautifully. So I had nothing to worry about. Right? Oh, how very wrong! I returned the following day to learn that my little "angels" had turned into raging devils in the hands of the substitute. The substitute vowed never to come near my class again. She was devastated, and so was I. How could this have happened? What had gone wrong? I learned the hard way that I had missed one crucial step. Yes, I had provided the substitute teacher with explicit instructions, but I had totally forgotten about the instructions for my students. So just as the poor, unsuspecting substitute teacher vowed never to enter my classroom doors again, I vowed never to let such a situation occur again should I be absent. The solution was quite simple, and it worked like a charm! The next time I had a meeting to attend, this is what I did, step by step:

+ I told my students I would be absent and that I would need for them to take over the classroom and help the substitute teacher. I made a big deal over the fact that I knew I could trust them, so I was not at all worried that things would not run smoothly.

+ I assigned roles to each student. For instance, one student had the task of welcoming the substitute and showing her where everything was located on my desk. Another student had the job of handing out the bellwork assignment to classmates as they entered the classroom. Another student had the job of giving the signal for quiet when the substitute was ready to begin and sharing that same signal with the substitute so that she could use it also. Another student had the job of explaining all of the daily procedures to the substitute. Another had the job of picking up assignments from students as they finished their work. I kept making up "jobs" until every student had one. One student even had the job of presenting the substitute with a small gift to show their appreciation at the end of the class period. Another had the job of "beginning the applause" after the gift was given. All students shared the job of thanking the substitute on the way out of the classroom, and one student was assigned to remind any student who forgot. Okay, you get the picture.

♦ On the day before I was to be absent, we practiced by pretending that I was the substitute. The students loved the idea, because now they were in charge of running the classroom and helping to make things easy on the substitute teacher. They had specific responsibilities, and they took pride in that fact.

♦ I wrote down all responsibilities of every student, and each got a copy. This would help to ensure that they would hold each other accountable or simply remind each other if one of them forgot an assigned job.

♦ We also discussed the fact that this same plan would remain in place if I were ever absent due to illness. For this, we kept an extra "gift" in the closet.

Results? I returned the day after my absence to find a two-page letter from the substitute. She said to PLEASE call her if I ever needed a substitute again. She went on to say that she had never witnessed anything like it. She was amazed at how helpful and cooperative the students were. "And can you believe that they actually clapped for me at the end of the class? I've never received applause in my life! And I believe that every single one of them stopped to thank me on the way out." You see, the students had played their roles so well that she didn't even realize that most of it had been rehearsed and that they were "supposed" to stop and thank her on the way out.

The students couldn't wait to brag about how well they had run the class without me! It worked for me every time I used it over the years, it worked for every teacher I shared it with, and it will work for you!

Instruction

> **"Our greatest glory is not in never falling, but in rising every time we fall."**
>
> Confucius

Learn to Recover Quickly

Teachers, even the best teachers, make mistakes. We are, after all, human. One of the differences between effective teachers and ineffective teachers is that effective teachers know how to recover from their mistakes quickly. When they make a mistake, they readily admit it. If at all possible, they correct it. And then they move on. Ineffective teachers try to hide behind defensiveness, thus making the mistake a bigger deal than it usually is and preventing themselves from earning the respect of their students.

When you say something you should not have said, or when you inadvertently hurt a child's feelings, or when you give incorrect information, apologize immediately and correct the mistake if possible. Acknowledge your mistake, and then let it go. By doing this, you will earn the respect of those you work with and those you teach, and you will be teaching others that mistakes, if handled appropriately, can provide wonderful opportunities for learning and growing.

Tip 29

Teach Students at "Their Level"

I have always been baffled by the age-old questions asked time and again by educators—"At what level should we teach students? Should we teach them at their own level or at grade level?" Well, think about this: When you first learned to speak, you learned at YOUR level. It didn't matter that other babies your age spoke sooner or later than you did. You had to be ready. You couldn't have possibly learned to speak at anyone else's level. So you learned at your level, and today you can speak. When you learned to walk, it was at YOUR level. It didn't matter that some babies walked as early as seven months and you did not walk until thirteen months. No one panicked. They simply waited until you were ready. You learned at your level, and today you can walk. And so it went for any skill you learned as you were growing up—that is, until you got to school. Then you were possibly expected to read before you were ready, which, of course, is impossible—but hey, lots of other kids your age could do it. And if you were forced to attempt skills at levels above your own, then you experienced failure, which, of course, bred more failure. The simple fact is that none of us can learn anything at anyone else's level. However, if we are taken from our level and moved forward, one step at a time, then there's no stopping us!

I have had the privilege of knowing, for many years, a teacher who believes that students must be taught at their own levels. She teaches in a middle school where the population is impoverished and most of the students are considered "at risk." Her students consist of "alternative" students—seventh graders who have been retained as many as three times, many of whom are 15 years old. Her task is to teach, in one school year, both the seventh and eighth grade curriculums to these students in order to prepare them for the eighth-grade statewide criterion-referenced test. If they pass the test, they move on to the ninth grade. Now remember that these students are considerably behind "typical" seventh-graders in their achievement. The task seems foreboding, and most teachers would say it's impossible. Are you ready for the results? This teacher's students have almost a 90 percent passing rate on the statewide test. In fact, their passing rate is above both the district and the state levels! How does this teacher do it? How does she take students who have trouble writing complete sentences and get them to write structured essays within less than eight months? Her answer? "I teach them at their own levels. If they can't write a sentence, even though they're 'supposed' to be able to write sentences at their age, I simply teach them how to write a sentence.

When they're ready, we move on to writing paragraphs and then eventually essays. I make sure that they experience nothing but success, and it becomes a habit—a way of thinking."

I guess it is true that "common sense is not necessarily common." If all teachers took all students from where they were and moved them forward to where they could be (as opposed to teaching them at the level they're "supposed" to be), the student achievement in our nation's schools would skyrocket!

Remember, we teach *students*. And the only way to teach students is *at their levels*!

"One of the most beneficial parts of mentoring for me was the opportunity to watch my mentor and others teach. I got to see the same things being taught that I was teaching in creative ways I'd never thought about. I had the opportunity to see different systems of excellent classroom management. I also got to see things I did *not* like and did *not* want to implement in my classroom."

Stephanie Blakeman,
Second-Year Teacher

Observe Other Teachers

Teaching continues to be a very "isolated" profession. We spend the majority of our time in our own classrooms and rarely see beyond our four walls! Yet collaboration has proven time and again to be very beneficial, rejuvenating, and enlightening for teachers. So why don't we do more of it? Some of our best ideas are "stolen" from other teachers. And the good news is that teachers are a very generous group of people, always happy to share their successes with others. Ask teachers how many opportunities they have had to observe other teachers teaching and they will tell you that these opportunities have been either rare or nonexistent. If you are a mentor, don't just observe the teacher you are mentoring. Allow that teacher to learn from observing you and others. Just as it's crucial that as teachers we model the skills we teach our students, so must mentors model good teaching for the teachers they're mentoring. If you are a new teacher, ask your administrator to schedule some time for you to observe your mentor and others. You'll be amazed at how much you will learn from watching others. Oh, and don't sell yourself short. Your mentor will also be amazed at how much there is to learn from watching you!

Teach Away

Teach, teach, teach away
Preach, preach all the day
You'd save your voice and I'd learn more, too
If you'd stop talking and let me do!

Annette L. Breaux,
No Adults Allowed

Refrain from "Lecturing"

Fact: Lecturing is one of the *least* effective means of instructing, yet it is one of the most often used! To make that point clear, let's imagine that you are learning a new skill—you are learning to swim. Your instructor seats you and 20 other novices in desks beside the pool. He lectures to you on swimming and you take notes. You literally hear everything there is to know about swimming because your instructor is an advanced swimmer. He knows his stuff! All of his information is accurate, so you are receiving "good" instruction. In fact, he even gets into the pool and models good swimming for you. After memorizing everything there is to know about swimming, you take the exam—a written test. You have put much time and effort into your studies, and you ace the exam. You are now a good swimmer. Right??? Well, if you're thinking that this is absolutely ridiculous, you are correct. We don't learn to swim by listening to great lectures on swimming. We learn to swim by swimming. We don't learn to drive a car by listening to informative lectures on driving. We learn by actually "doing" the driving. So it is in life, and so it is in the classroom. That is not to say that there is never a place for lecturing, but lecturing does not teach us to "do" anything. Great writers did not become great writers because they listened to lectures and memorized all of the "rules." Good readers did not become good readers by listening to lectures on reading. They became adept at their skills through "doing." Great historians did not become great historians by listening to lectures and memorizing history. They actually dove in and swam around in history. I've often heard it said, "The one who does the doing does the learning." I am yet to hear it said that the one who can listen really intently to great lectures does the learning. Perhaps I missed that particular lecture!

FACT: I know of no adults who owe their successes to the efficacy of a textbook but of many who owe their successes to the influence of a teacher.

Refrain from "Textbook Teaching"

No, I am not suggesting that you throw away your trusty textbooks. I can think of very few teachers who do not use textbooks. They are valuable resources. Ah, that is the key—they are "resources." I recently witnessed a conversation in a faculty lounge. It went like this: "Can you believe that they've adopted this new textbook? I can't teach from that. I'm going to continue to use the textbook I've been using. I'm not about to change all of my lesson plans because of a new textbook. Also, this textbook has more content, and it's too much material to cover in one school year. I can cover the textbook I'm using now in exactly one school year." This brought to mind another teacher who used to have his students, on the first day of school, actually "sit" on their textbooks. He would then say, "Okay, we have now 'covered' the textbook." This is not to say that he did not use the textbook as a resource in his teaching. He did. But he used it as a supplement to his teaching. The textbook did not make his instructional decisions. He made his instructional decisions based on the needs of his students. So should we all. Most districts have very specific curriculums, based on content standards and benchmarks, from which teachers are expected to teach. No textbook has an exact correlation to any district's curriculum. However, when selecting textbooks, districts consider those that have the closest correlation to their own curriculums. Often, however, teachers see the textbook as the definitive curriculum. They literally cover the book from beginning to end, neglecting to teach much of the district's curriculum. The effective teacher begins with the curriculum and then determines the best resources available to teach that curriculum. The ineffective teacher depends on textbooks to tell him what to teach, when to teach it, what questions to ask the students, what answers the students should give, and to provide him with formatted tests and answer keys to everything he has "covered." A good question to ask yourself is this: "If I gave the same test next week that I am giving this week, would the students pass?" If your answer is "no," then you are "covering" material, not teaching it. You are simply "loaning" the students the information from the textbook until the test, when they "give it back" to you.

A textbook should be used as a teaching tool, one of many resources. Another good question to ask yourself is this: "If all of the textbooks were removed from my classroom, would I be able to continue my teaching?" If your answer if "no," then you are relying too heavily on the textbook in your instruction. Remember, textbooks are resources. We teach *students,* not textbooks.

"To educate a man in mind and not in morals is to educate a menace to society."

Theodore Roosevelt

Teach Social Skills

To begin with, assume nothing! Don't expect that students will come to you with perfect manners. Don't assume that your students will always know right from wrong. Don't assume that students will work cooperatively and get along with others. Don't assume that students will even know how to make proper eye contact when speaking to others. Some will, but many won't. I often hear it said that parents should be responsible for teaching social skills. I'm not arguing that point at all. But the fact remains that many students learn good social skills from their parents and many do not. If we are truly to call ourselves "educators," then we must educate the whole person. So where do we find the time to "fit it in" to the already overloaded curriculum? We begin, of course, by being good models. That takes no time at all. And then we weave proper social skills into everything that we teach. I once knew a teacher who constantly complained about her students having no manners and not being able to get along with others. When I asked her how she incorporated social skills into her teaching, she answered, "I don't. It's not my job." Upon observing her, I noticed that not only did she refrain from teaching social skills, but she also refrained from modeling them. She was loud, she displayed negative body language, she never said "please" or "thank you," and her lessons were boring. Students worked alone, and it's tough to learn social skills without the benefit of social interaction! Out of curiosity, I observed the same ill-behaved students with another teacher. Guess what? They were no longer ill-behaved. This teacher did the following:

- She modeled good social skills from the moment she greeted the students at the classroom door.
- She was very polite and pleasant with her students.
- She thanked students often.
- She took a few minutes here and there, when giving directions for a group activity, to talk about what proper behavior in the activity would "look" like.
- She had students constantly involved with one another in learning activities.

The list goes on, but the bottom line was that she did almost the exact opposite of what the "complaining" teacher did. And guess what? She got the exact opposite behavior from her students.

I went back to the first teacher and said, "Let's try an experiment. I think that maybe your students are a little lacking in their social skills." "A little lacking?" she asked. "Try ground zero!" "Okay," I said. "I'm going to help you to turn that around, if you're willing to give it a try." "Sure," she said. "I'll try anything." Without telling her what I had observed in the other teacher's classroom, I simply gave her a list of what the other teacher was doing. I had her do five basic things:

1. Greet students at the door every day as if you are genuinely happy to see them. Fake it if you have to.

2. Speak in a soft, pleasant tone, and don't let them make you lose your temper at any cost.

3. Make a concerted effort to thank your students for every appropriate behavior.

4. Explain what proper behavior looks like well in advance of any and all activities.

5. Start enabling more student interaction, both with the teacher and with classmates.

We agreed that I would observe her every day for five days—one school week. Following each lesson, I would provide feedback and we would discuss any positive changes in student behavior. By the end of the fifth day, she was a "new" person and her students were "new" students. To this day, she thanks me every time she sees me for helping her to change her approach. She never once said, "Thanks for helping my students to behave more appropriately." Instead, she realized that her own modeling and approach with her students was what made the difference. So teach and model good social skills, and your students will amaze you!

> "There is something that is much more scarce, something finer far, something rarer than ability. It is the ability to recognize ability."
>
> Elbert Hubbard

Focus on Students' Strengths

Think of two of your most challenging students. Get them clearly in your mind. Now list all of their strengths along with all of their weaknesses. My hunch is that you were able to list many more weaknesses than strengths. But knowing that success truly does breed success, we need to turn our thinking around and begin focusing on the strengths of each student. A teacher once insisted to me that she had three students who made her entire life miserable. I asked her to tell me about the strengths of each student, and she answered, "Not one of them has any strengths at all." No wonder these students were causing problems in the classroom. They were considered to be "hopeless" by their teacher. The fact is that every student—yes, every single student—possesses lots of strengths. Sometimes we have to search a little harder and dig a little deeper to find strengths in some, but the strengths are there. As I often like to do, I observed these three students, all of whom happened to be boys, in the teacher's classroom, and then I followed the three boys into another teacher's classroom. Seeing that these students experienced "personality" changes in the second teacher's classroom, I decided to speak to the second teacher. I asked her to tell me about each boy and to list his strengths and his weaknesses. Her comments went as follows: "Wendell is very polite. He does struggle with the content, but he gives 100 percent to his efforts. He has wonderful leadership abilities, and he has a heart of gold. His penmanship is meticulous, and his work is always done so neatly. He's also a very good listener." The comments about the other two boys were very similar in that they focused on strengths as opposed to weaknesses. I then asked the teacher what she did differently with Wendell, because he had trouble grasping the content. She answered, "I provide remediation activities for him, and then he catches on because he's so willing and determined. I also give him lots of responsibilities around the classroom, because he handles responsibility very well. I just do things that help to ensure his success every day, and the growth in him has been phenomenal!"

As expressed in Tip 80, life truly is what we focus on. If you want students to succeed, then focus on their strengths. It's really that simple!

Tip 35

Question: Do your students know how to work together—to cooperate with one another? If not, it's time to teach them.

Allow and Encourage Students to Work Cooperatively

Much research has been conducted on the power of cooperative learning. The results have been consistent: Students who engage in cooperative learning activities develop problem-solving skills, develop better social skills, and achieve at higher levels. So why is it that so many teachers, of all grade levels, tend to avoid the idea of having students work together in cooperative learning environments? Once again, we must look back at classroom management. The following are actual teachers' answers to the question, "Why don't you use cooperative learning activities in your classroom?"

- ♦ I've tried letting my students work together, and they just can't get along with one another.
- ♦ I put my students in groups, and one person does all of the work.
- ♦ I don't want to hold back the stronger students because of the lack of understanding on the parts of the weaker students.
- ♦ Cooperative learning equals chaos. I want structure and order in my classroom.
- ♦ Today's students don't possess the social skills required to work cooperatively. They simply cannot work together.
- ♦ I tried cooperative learning once, and my students argued with one another.
- ♦ I like a quiet classroom, and I'm not about to put my students in groups where all they will do is talk.

Notice that in all of the above answers, the issues of order, structure, noise, lack of on-task behavior, and chaos are evident. Again, all point to problems in classroom management. Yes, the above fears can become realities, but *not* in true cooperative learning conducted in a well-managed environment. The key here is structure. Though it is impossible to do justice to describing cooperative learning completely here, I aim to provide enough of the overall premise underlying the success of its use in the classroom to encourage those reading this to familiarize themselves with some of the vast literature on cooperative learning.

In a nutshell, this is what true cooperative learning looks like:

- Students are assigned to groups consisting of various personality types and ability levels.
- Each student in the group has a specific job in carrying out the overall charge of the group.
- All activities are highly structured.
- Appropriate behaviors in the group are taught, modeled, and practiced.
- "Noise" levels are under control, and all "noise" is structured "noise."
- Students of all ability levels are challenged to think critically and to solve problems cooperatively, just like in the "real" world.
- Procedures for each aspect of group interaction are clearly established, from day one.
- Students are involved in the group's mission, and they experience high levels of success.

Remember that before implementing any type of cooperative group activities, classroom management must be in place. It is often stated that any teacher who argues against encouraging students to work cooperatively has never encouraged students to work cooperatively. Life is about cooperation. We simply cannot expect students to come to us possessing all of the skills they need in order to work cooperatively with others. That's why they need us! We're here to teach them. Let's do our jobs.

Do you ever hear a student ask, "Why do we have to know this?" If you do, then it's a red flag to you that you have not made that critical "real life" connection!

Relate Lessons to Real Life

Aristotle said, "All knowledge is relational." In other words, in order for us to learn anything new, we must have something we already "know" with which to connect the new skill. When work "makes sense" to us, we have a purpose for doing it. If it does not seem meaningful, we close our minds to it. After all, what's the point in learning something that has no meaning in our lives? I often hear students say that they "hate" English or they "hate" reading. However, I have yet to encounter students who "hate" English or reading when it comes to reading the menu at their favorite fast-food restaurant or when they receive a note from a friend. Let's drive this point home with a classroom experience that most, if not all of us, have had. We all learned about "nouns" in a similar fashion. In fact, our experiences were so similar, no matter where we went to school, that it's almost frightening. Think back. The lesson was taught in the following way: The teacher had us take out our English books and open to page 27. The title, atop the page, was "Nouns." We had to write that title in our notebooks. Then, beneath the title was a definition, usually written in red or blue. The definition read, "A noun names a person, place, or thing." We then copied that definition into our notebooks. The teacher had us name different people, places, and things, and we categorized those. Then we completed "Exercise A" where we had to underline the nouns. Following this, we did "Exercise B." We next wrote our own sentences, identifying the nouns as people, places, or things. And, of course, we had a worksheet to take home and complete. The test was on Friday. Sounding familiar yet? Well, is it any wonder that kids claim to "hate" English? What does any of this have to do with their lives, other than the fact that they have to pass the test on Friday? That, by the way, is *not* a real-life connection.

Okay, now let's consider a completely different scenario. Notice that it takes no extra time or work. It simply involves using a little common sense. The teacher begins the lesson by saying, "You don't need to take a thing out right now. Angela, tell me about something you did yesterday, but do not name any people, any places, or any things." Angela says, "My brother…" And the teacher interrupts and says, "Oops, your brother is a person." Then she says, " went to the mall…" and the teacher interrupts and says, "No, the mall is a place." And Angela is having difficulty. The teacher then asks another student to help by telling about something he did yesterday, without, of course, naming any people, places, or things. Within seconds, the students figure out that the task is impossible. The teacher says, "Oh, so you're telling me that without people, places, and things, you cannot speak in a way that makes sense? Okay, then write a sentence about something you did yesterday without naming any people, places, or things. I'll walk around and help you." As the students get busy, the teacher walks around and has each student cross out any word that is a person, place, or thing. When everyone has finished, they are to read their sentences to the class. Tim reads his. It sounds like this: "A it the at the in the." The students laugh at their sentences and realize that writing makes no sense either without including people, places, or things. The teacher then says, "So you're telling me that you could not speak or write or even *think* without people, places, and things? They're called "nouns," by the way. Okay, so how would your life be different if you could not communicate orally or in writing? A discussion follows as to the importance of these parts of speech—nouns. Do you see how the teacher has gotten the students to understand the real-life connection and its importance in their everyday lives? That's teaching! Afterward, if the teacher chooses to use the textbook definition and to have the students complete exercises A and B, it's okay, because the relevance of what they're doing has been established! I'll bet that some of you reading this are thinking to yourself, "I've never even thought about nouns that way before!" That's because it was never taught to you in that way, so you never really stopped to analyze the importance of every facet of our language.

As you rethink your own teaching methods, you will probably realize that it's difficult, at times, to come up with the "real-life" connection in teaching certain skills. Again, it's because it was never explained to you in that way. But how can we, as teachers, expect our students to "buy in" to something for which they see no meaning? We can't! So make that real-life connection with every skill you teach. And if you ever come across a skill that truly has no real-life connection, then we should remove that skill from the curriculum!

> ### The Life of a Kid
>
> *Go to school all the day*
> *Do your homework before you play*
> *Be sure to be in bed by eight*
> *Up at dawn, do not be late*
> *Tonight inside my bed I lay*
> *A very selfish prayer I pray*
> *I beg and plead with Mr. Sun*
> *Shine longer tomorrow—I need to have fun.*
>
> Annette L. Breaux,
> *No Adults Allowed*

Avoid Homework Overload

I often hear parents complain about how much homework their children have. I often hear children complain about having to do their homework. And I most often hear teachers complaining about how their students do *not* turn in homework assignments. No one seems to be too crazy about the idea of homework, yet some teachers keep piling it on. Often, a student has several teachers, all of whom assign homework. Imagine that a student has six teachers and each teacher assigns homework activities that require about twenty minutes of work. That's two hours of homework, *if* the student understands the concepts and does not struggle. So if a student leaves home at 7:30 AM and returns home at 4:00 PM and immediately gets busy doing homework, where does he find time to play? Where's the time to just be a kid? And let's not forget that many students are involved in after-school activities that require hours of their time each week. Is it any wonder that parents get upset? And is it any wonder that many students do not turn in their homework assignments?

I am not opposed to the idea of homework, but as the saying goes, "Everything in moderation." Students spend between seven and eight hours a day at school. Does it make sense to send them home with hours of work yet ahead of them? I've always felt that if I taught from bell to bell and worked hard every day with my students, then homework would not become a nightly event. In fact, for some teachers, homework is only assigned occasionally. Much research has been conducted and much controversy has arisen involving the "homework" question. Do students "need" homework? Does homework improve achievement? Does homework foster responsibility? Should homework affect student grades? The list goes on and on, and so does the research. To date, the jury is still out on the homework issue.

Therefore, my suggestions to you are as follows:

- If you feel that homework is necessary, then assign it, but do so in moderation.

- If you are one of several teachers who teach the same students, get together with those teachers and take turns assigning homework.

- When you do assign homework, make sure that the assignments are interesting, meaningful, and doable. Students are much more likely to complete such assignments.

- Do not make a big deal out of missed homework assignments. (The old trick of doubling the amount, tripling the amount, etc. for students who do not turn in assignments has never worked. If they didn't do it once, they're not likely to do it twice.)

- Remember that all students do not go home to Ward and June Cleaver households.

And most importantly, remember that you teach children—yes, even high school students are "children," and they need a break from their studies. For that matter, let's hope there's a little bit of a child left in all of us. If we could remember that, we'd all be a lot happier and a lot less stressed!

> "My heart is singing for joy this morning. A miracle has happened! The light of understanding has shown upon my little pupil's mind, and behold, all things are changed."

> Anne Sullivan

Model the Skills You Teach

It is truly beyond comprehension how one individual, a teacher, Anne Sullivan, was able to unlock the extraordinary potentials hidden inside of a little girl who could not see, speak, or hear—Helen Keller. How does one even begin? What incredible patience must one possess? The answer, for Anne Sullivan, was to begin at the very beginning, resolved to uncover the spirit, the intelligence, the profound thoughts and feelings, the talents, the gifts, and the beauty that embodied one of the most amazing women in history. And to think that Anne Sullivan accomplished all of this without lecturing, without worksheets! Anne Sullivan "modeled" every skill she taught, and then Helen practiced and practiced and practiced with her teacher's guidance until she was ready to attempt the skill on her own. Fortunately, very few of us will ever teach a student with as many challenges as those that faced Helen Keller, yet all of us should model every skill we teach. This is how students begin to understand a concept—by "seeing" what it looks like. Interestingly yet unfortunately, teachers often overlook modeling when teaching a new skill. They tell, students listen, and then they send the students off on their own. Yet, students have never actually "seen" what they're supposed to perform. A common example is as follows: A teacher is teaching the students to write a descriptive paragraph. The teacher conducts a review of basic paragraph writing, the teacher and students discuss some descriptive words, the teacher describes the process of writing a descriptive paragraph, and then the students are given a topic on which to write a descriptive paragraph. Notice that the teacher never actually "modeled" the process of writing a descriptive paragraph for the students. Students need to "see" what the process looks like and listen as the teacher "thinks aloud" and models the thought process that goes into writing the paragraph. Then, the teacher and students should write a class paragraph, thinking it through together. This way, when the students are to perform the task on their own, they will have a mental picture of the process along with some guided practice under their belts. Imagine teaching someone to swim without ever demonstrating what swimming "looks" like. Imagine teaching someone to ride a bike without ever demonstrating what bike riding "looks" like. That would be ludicrous, yet we do it every day in the classroom! Teaching, in any form, requires modeling. So model, model, model, and when the "light of understanding" shows upon your pupils' minds, all will be changed.

> **"You can do anything with children if you only play with them."**
>
> Prince Otto von Bismarck

Make Learning Fun

While I was conducting a presentation for high school teachers and university personnel on effective teaching, a college professor volunteered the following: "When I walked into the training today and learned of the kinds of activities that were going to be conducted, I almost walked out. I thought it was going to be 'elementary.' However, after participating in the activities and having fun doing so, I realized that if I could have fun, then maybe it was okay for my students to have fun as opposed to just sitting and listening to my daily lectures. Besides that, maybe I'd even have fun teaching!" In response, a high school teacher enthusiastically added, "I do what are considered 'elementary' activities with my high school students every day, and they love it!" When I asked what she meant by 'elementary' activities, she explained that she used lots of cooperative learning, lots of learning games, lots of hands-on activities, lots of group discussion, and very little lecture. "My students love to come to my class, because they have so much fun and they experience so much success." A very interesting discussion ensued where we discussed the fact that students learn best when they are having fun. "So do adults!" added one of the participants.

Too often, I encounter teachers who think that teaching and learning should always be "serious business." Their demeanors are serious, their classrooms are serious places, their students are bored out of their minds, and discipline problems are evident. Not very conducive to inspiring students to achieve! The fact is that we all learn best when the learning environment is interesting, exciting, and inviting. Some teachers are afraid to allow their students to have "fun" in their classrooms, for fear of losing control of discipline. This is a mistake, in that 'fun' and 'chaos' are not synonymous. Chaos is a classroom management problem. If classroom management is well established, there will be no chaos. Good teachers know that in the most effective learning environments, classroom management is established, students are actively involved in the learning, lessons and activities are both highly structured and of high interest to students, and students are enjoying the learning process. Yes, they are having fun!

Remember—Taking teaching seriously and treating teaching as strictly serious business are two very different things. So lighten up, add zest to your lessons, and watch your students' achievement increase. Your students will enjoy their learning, you will enjoy your teaching, and you will all have fun.

Tip 40

> I hear and I forget.
> I see and I remember.
> I do and I understand.

> Chinese Proverb

Encourage Active Student Participation

Think of the following classroom scenario: You are a student in a classroom on a typical day—typical, because every day is the same. You walk into class, you sit at your desk, and the teacher tells you to open your textbook. The teacher lectures, and you take notes. You read a chapter, and then you answer the questions at the end of the chapter. You complete lots of worksheets, and when you finish those, you complete more worksheets. You use your glossary to define 20 or so vocabulary words, all of which must be memorized, along with your notes, for Friday's test. The teacher does most of the talking in the classroom, and you do most of the sitting. You are expected to pay attention, be interested, keep quiet, and master your lessons. Now, imagine going through this same routine every single day for 180 days! And now answer the following questions:

- Where is the actual "teaching" in what I have just described?
- How much "sitting still" can any student endure?
- Where's the "doing" on the part of the students?
- Where are students actually solving problems or thinking critically?
- When have reading a chapter and answering questions at the end of the chapter ever increased *any* student's achievement?

Now consider another scenario. You are a student. You walk into class every day, never knowing what awaits you, for no day is ever the same. You have been deeply involved in studying the Civil War. There has been much research conducted by the teacher and students together. There have been interesting class discussions, where students have been allowed to interact with the research and voice their opinions. Today, you are assigned to groups. Each group has a different assignment. You will all be writing about your thoughts on the war from different viewpoints. The teacher teaches and models the activity for the students so that they are all clear on what today's task will entail. One group will write from the viewpoint of a Confederate soldier. Another will write from the viewpoint of a Union soldier. Another will write from the viewpoint of a slave owner and another from the viewpoint of a slave. Still another will be from the viewpoint of the mother of a soldier. In order to complete your assignments, you will be using research—your own research. The teacher will interact with all groups as they work on their assignments. Then, each group will present its findings and original writings to the class. Discussion on each presentation will follow. Now, can you see the difference in this scenario and the previous one? Did you recognize the teaching here, the active student participation, the interest level, the opportunities for meaningful learning, and the lack of boredom? In which class would you prefer to be a student?

To rephrase the Chinese proverb above, "What I hear in the classroom goes in one ear and out the other, what I see in the classroom I tend to remember seeing, but what I actually have to do, I learn, and the learning sticks, because I understand." Have your students *do* as opposed to having them *endure*!

> **"Too often we give our students answers to remember rather than problems to solve."**
>
> Roger Lewin

Challenge Students to Think Critically

I recently met a little boy at a friend's house. Being an educator, I asked him about school. He enthusiastically told me that his favorite subject was math. He went on to tell me that he knew all of his multiplication facts very well. I began "quizzing" him. Sure enough, he knew the "answers." When I asked him what was 4 x 4, he readily answered, "16." Then I asked, "What does that mean?" Again, he answered "16." I realized that the student had no concept of what multiplication actually "meant." So the teacher in me broke into a quick "lesson." After explaining the concept of multiplication, he said, "Oh! Is that what that means? Do you mean that if I have four groups of people with four people in each group, that's the same as saying 4 x 4 = 16? I never knew that!" He immediately grabbed a deck of cards and started arranging them into groups and coming up with his own multiplication facts. I then had to sit with him for the next two hours and share in his enthusiasm, ignoring the group of adults with whom I had previously been visiting. But that was okay, because, as all teachers know, when the light bulb goes on in a child's mind, there's no turning it off!

The point I'm trying to make is that we, as teachers, often assume too much. Just because a student knows an answer or can memorize a given piece of information, we assume that he "understands." This is usually not the case. Knowing information and being able to apply that information by thinking critically to solve problems are two different things.

I can remember the day that I figured out why we spent so much time in school diagramming sentences. I was always fairly adept at the skill, but I never really understood its purpose. Then one day, the light bulb went on, and I realized what the skill was all about. I couldn't believe I had "missed" that somewhere along the line. I now had a totally newfound understanding of the English language!

Critical thinking involves problem solving, which fosters a true understanding of a concept. Think about this: How many times, in your adult life, have you had to regurgitate the important battles of any of the many wars in which America has been involved? You "learned" them in your schooling, but unless you are a history buff, you probably don't remember them, nor do you need to in order to get along in life! What was important was to understand the reasons behind the wars—how and why they began, how and why we, as a nation, became involved, how people's lives were affected because of wars, and how life as we know it today is influenced by the history that preceded it.

Recently, as a "fun" experiment, I took a group of 32 ninth graders and asked them to identify pronouns in a given set of sentences. With three exceptions, they were all able to complete the task successfully and accurately. Then I asked, "Now why do we have pronouns in our language, and how would life be different without them?" I received blank stares. Nothing. No answers. Then I had each of them attempt to tell me something about themselves without using pronouns. (You may want to attempt it yourself before you read on.) Within a minute, the students suddenly saw how awkward the language would be without the use of pronouns. "Oh, I get it!" said one of the students. "Pronouns help to make the language less awkward and more efficient!" Then I took the three students who had had a little trouble with pronouns, provided quick remediation, and once again, the light bulbs went on, because the concept was now clear.

We need to make a concerted effort in our teaching to stop doling out facts and start encouraging students to think critically. Once they understand a concept, the facts become meaningful. This is the kind of thinking that arouses student interest, that encourages them to delve deeply into concepts, that urges them to remain in a continual state of questioning.

How much sense would it make to take a written exam in swimming in order to determine whether you are a good swimmer?

Use Authentic Means of Assessment

There is much debate in the field of education and lots of controversy over the best means of assessing student work. Without any research and without any controversy, I will put the whole idea of authentic assessment into perspective for you. The word "authentic" means "real" or "valid." Therefore, authentic assessment is a valid way of knowing whether or not your students have attained a particular skill. In the question above, even the slightest bit of common sense will tell you that assessing the skill of swimming by using a written test is ludicrous. Authentic assessment of this skill would require that the student actually swim. So it is with any skill that we teach. In order to determine a student's knowledge of particular vocabulary, regurgitating memorized definitions tells us nothing. The student must actually be able to "use" the vocabulary words. A written test on the scientific method is not valid if the student is only required to list the steps in the scientific method. He must be able to apply the method to a given experiment. Giving a set of questions based on a reading story that has been discussed all week in class is really a test in "memory" as opposed to a test in reading comprehension. In order to know if students can truly comprehend what they read, they must be tested with unfamiliar text.

If you want to know if a person can cook, then have the person cook something. Again, that's common sense. So, apply that same logic in your classroom. In assessing student work, decide what it is that you want to assess, and then assess it in a way that is "real" and "valid." It's really that simple!

Tip 43

> ## "Students welcome any change from routine."
>
> William Glasser, M.D.

Vary Your Teaching Strategies

It is human nature to be intrigued by "the element of surprise." Students, in particular, respond favorably to teachers who keep them intrigued, wondering what exciting thing will happen next. Let's be clear, however, that we are referring to teaching strategies and not to classroom management strategies. Regarding routines and procedures in the classroom—how to enter the room, when to focus attention on the teacher, how to pass in papers, how to ask for permission to speak, what to do when there is a fire drill, etc.—there is no room for "the element of surprise!" These things should remain consistent, so as not to become confusing or chaotic. But regarding teaching strategies, spice it up. As the saying goes, "Variety is the spice of life." Successful teachers know this, and they use every available opportunity to capitalize on this with their students.

We can all recall sitting in classrooms where the only variety that we noticed was the change of the date on the calendar every day. It was the same old same old, day in and day out. We walked into class, we opened our textbooks, the teacher lectured, we took notes, and—you know the rest of the routine. In speaking to a middle-school student about his favorite teacher, he said, "What's really great about Mr. Carter's class is that we never know what to expect. Some days we walk into class and he's dressed as the character we'll be discussing. Other days, he's hurrying us into the room saying, 'You won't believe what I have in store for you today.' The man is so full of energy that we all seem to 'catch' it. He keeps us moving all the time. Some days he wears us out. It's always something different—not that old boring lecture stuff that we get from some of our other teachers. All the kids love him, and even the tough kids behave in Mr. Carter's class."

I think you'll agree that this student's words say a lot. However, the icing on the cake was when a fifth-grade student described her "favorite" teacher and the importance of variety in teaching. She said, with a giant smile on her face, "Ms. Barton is like chicken, but the good kind." "What do you mean?" I asked. "Well, I'll tell you what the bad kind is first. With some teachers, going to their class is like eating plain old chicken, cooked the same way, every single day. Even if you like it at first, you get tired of eating chicken cooked the same way all the time. But in Ms. Barton's class, some days it's fried chicken, some days it's barbecued chicken, some days it's chicken soup, some days it's baked chicken, and some days it's chicken nuggets, but it's always cooked really well—and all the kids like it, so we eat a lot of it, and we never get tired of it, because it always changes." "Wow!" I thought. "From the mouths of babes."

Vary your teaching strategies. Move quickly from exciting explanations to inviting discussions to interesting hands-on learning activities to class projects to student demonstrations of skills, and so on. Change your routine so that your lessons do not always look the same. Do you know how many ways there are to prepare chicken?

> **"A smooth sea never made a skillful mariner."**
>
> English Proverb

Make Decisions Based on What's Best for Students

Here is a quiz to measure your ability to make decisions based on what's best for students, as opposed to what's easiest for you. It will include three questions, for which you are to select the most appropriate answers.

1. It's Friday. You're tired. No, you're exhausted. You just learned that your principal is away at a meeting. Your science lesson plans state that your students will be learning the difference between acids and bases. You have some wonderful experiments planned, all of which will require a great deal of effort on your part. You have some wonderful activities planned, but all will require a great deal of effort on your part. You suddenly remember that you have a video where "Gerty Guesser, the Science Professor" experiments with acids and bases. The video would "eat up" the entire class period. What do you do?

    (a) Show the video

    (b) Teach as you had intended

2. You are giving a test in English on the use of alliteration. The textbook has a nice little multiple-choice test, complete with answer key. Your grading time will be minimal. What do you do?

    (a) Give the textbook test

    (b) Have the students write a paragraph using alliteration

3. With your students, you are studying World War II and its impact on America's economy. The textbook has a very informative chapter on this topic. It's so informative, in fact, that you consider just letting the students read the chapter and answer the questions at the end of the chapter. What do you do?

    (a) Assign the chapter and the questions

    (b) Use the textbook information to engage the students in meaningful discussions and critical thinking activities.

If you answered "b" for all three questions, then you have the ability to recognize the kind of teaching that benefits students. Pat yourself on the back. You are making a difference.

As discussed in Tip 22, teaching is hard work. There will be days when you are exhausted and will be tempted to take the easy way out. It's human nature. However, don't give in to the temptation. Do what's best for students, always!

Tip 45

Professionalism: Attitudes and Behaviors of Effective Teachers

> **"Character is much easier kept than recovered."**
>
> Thomas Paine

Maintain a Positive Reputation

Every teacher, in every classroom, on every school campus has a "reputation." If you have taught more than one week, you have a reputation. Students learn, very quickly, who the "nice" teachers are, who the "screamers" are, who gives the most homework, who "cares" the most, who holds the record for office referrals, etc. Parents judge the reputations of teachers based on what their children tell them. And teachers know the reputations of their counterparts also. You do not have to observe a teacher in the classroom to make a fairly accurate determination of that teacher's character and effectiveness in the classroom. You can watch teachers take their classes to lunch and tell whether management is in place; you can watch teachers interact with children on the school grounds and know what kind of rapport exists; you can walk down the hallways and know who's teaching; and you can listen to their conversations with others and learn a lot about their attitudes, their professionalism, and their overall effectiveness as teachers. Also, whether you want to or not, you will hear students talking about their teachers. No teacher wants to have a negative reputation, yet many do. The best way to steer clear of a negative reputation is not to establish one in the first place, because once you have one, it's extremely difficult to change it. So, teach from your heart, treat your students with dignity, carry yourself as a professional at all times, be the most enthusiastic person you know, and wear your positive reputation proudly!

Tip 46

The Cookie Thief

A woman was waiting at an airport one night,
With several long hours before her flight.
She hunted for a book in the airport shop,
Bought a bag of cookies and found a place to drop.
She was engrossed in her book, but happened to see,
That the man beside her, as bold as could be,
Grabbed a cookie or two from the bag between,
Which she tried to ignore to avoid a scene.
She read, munched cookies, and watched the clock
As the gutsy "cookie thief" diminished her stock
She was getting more irritated as the minutes ticked by
Thinking, "If I wasn't so nice, I'd blacken his eye!"
With each cookie she took, he took one too.
When only one was left, she wondered what he'd do.
With a smile on his face and a nervous laugh,
He took the last cookie and broke it in half.
He offered her half, as he ate the other.
She snatched it from him and thought, "Oh, brother!
This guy has some nerve and he's also rude.
Why, he didn't even show any gratitude!"
She had never known when she had been so galled,
And sighed with relief when her flight was called.
She gathered her belongings and headed for the gate
Refusing to look back at that "thieving ingrate."
She boarded the plane and sank in her seat,
Then sought her book which was almost complete.
As she reached in her baggage, she gasped with surprise.
There was her bag of cookies in front of her eyes!
"If mine are here," she moaned with despair,
"Then the others were his and he tried to share!"
Too late to apologize, she realized with grief,
That she was the rude one, the ingrate, the thief!

Valerie Cox

Do Not Fall Prey to Victimization

As you read the poem "The Cookie Thief," you soon realize that the woman, who seems a victim at first, is only a victim in her mind. Her perception of the situation is leading her to feel victimized. She is not a victim of the alleged "cookie thief."

Likewise, teachers are not victims of their jobs! We all picked our jobs. We proudly presented our credentials and interviewed for jobs that were offered to us. We then signed our names on the dotted lines of our contracts. We chose this profession. At any time, we are free to choose another. So how can we be victims of something we have chosen and continue to choose? We can't be! Yet, often you will hear conversations that sound something like this: "Can you believe what they're asking us to do? What do they think we are—superhuman?" And here's another common scenario: "If I could get rid of five students in my class, my life would be so wonderful. I think they gave me those students on purpose. And I'm sorry, but it's impossible to teach when you've got students acting like animals in your classroom. And don't bother sending them to the office, because nothing will be done. They just send them right back." And one more: "It must be wonderful for them to sit in an ivory tower barking out orders while we're killing ourselves in our classrooms. And to think that administrators get paid more than we do! What a joke, and what a waste of money!"

Do not let yourself fall prey to victimization! It's a dangerous road that leads to frustration, anger, self-righteousness, and all that is negative and harmful, not only to ourselves, but also to the children whose lives we continue to influence daily.

Remember, we all picked our jobs! We are not victims, but rather are those in whose hands society has entrusted its hopes and dreams for the future.

FACT: Circumstances don't 'make' the teacher.
Circumstances 'reveal' the teacher.

Choose Your Reactions

As has often been said, we have very *little* control over our circumstances, but we have very *much* control over how we choose to react to those circumstances. In the classroom, students will work diligently at determining who you are as a person and as a teacher. They will try to make you stop, stare up at the ceiling, and lose your patience. They will try to see if they can make you clench your teeth as you speak in an angry tone. They will even try to see how far they can make the vein stick out on the side of your neck! Don't give in. Be aware of the fact that you can always choose your reactions, in any situation.

I know of a teacher who always gets assigned the "problem" students. She teaches the ones no one else wants to teach, because of their prior histories of misbehavior. But this teacher knows how to choose her reactions very carefully. Each year, she welcomes the opportunity to teach the "un-teach-ables." She treats them with dignity, with patience, and with respect. She has high expectations for all of them. Oh yes, they "try" her at first. It happens every year. But the fact that she never gives them the reactions they're seeking soon neutralizes them. When they realize that she will not lose her temper, that she will not stop believing in them, and that she will do anything to make them successful, they stop trying to evoke negative responses from her. It works every year, as her record has shown. And her influence on her students is profound, as her students will gladly tell you.

Remember, your circumstances will never *determine* who you are as a teacher, but rather your reactions to those circumstances will most definitely *reveal*, to students, to parents, to coworkers, and to yourself, the kind of teacher you are and the kind of person you are. Choose your reactions!

> "If we had no faults of our own, we would not take so much pleasure in noticing those of others."
>
> Duc de La Rochefoucald

Don't Let Negative Coworkers Affect You

Fact: If there are more than three people on your school's faculty, then chances are good that there's a negative faction! This is not, in any way, to suggest that the majority of teachers are negative individuals. They're not. But one negative individual can have a tremendous negative influence on other coworkers. And, to date, I have yet to find a faculty that has been spared of a few negative coworkers.

As teachers, we all stand at a fork in the road where we are faced with a very important decision. We can choose to go "left"—fitting in and falling prey—or we can choose to go "right"—doing what's best for students, the only way! The fact is that you will not be alone on either path you choose. One way, however, is more difficult. It takes more guts. Which way is that? The "right" way. Let's look at what you'll get on each path.

If you go "right" and do what's best for students, there are pros and cons:

- *Pros*: Your classroom will be an exciting place, student achievement will rise, student self-esteem will rise, you will be highly respected by respectable educators and students, and your contribution to society will be immeasurable.

- *Cons*: You will work hard, and you will run the risk of being scrutinized by the people who chose to go "left."

- *Final destination*: You will be a happy, successful, hard-working, contributing, truly effective, highly qualified, and highly respected teacher who touches lives and makes a difference.

If you go "left" and choose to fit in and fall prey, there are pros and cons:

- *Pros*: All the negative people will like you, you will be allowed to gripe all you want, your workload will be lightened by the overuse of worksheets, busy work, and time-fillers, and you will experience the bliss of denial by simply blaming society, parents, administration, and your students, conveniently forgetting that YOU have total control, with very few exceptions, over what goes on in your classroom.

♦ *Cons*: You will very likely struggle with management and discipline—but it will at least give you something more to gripe about, you will know all the latest gossip, your cynical attitude will breed resentment in students, respectable educators will have no respect for you, and last, but definitely not least, you may figure out one day that you've taken the wrong road, and you'll be sorry.

♦ *Final destination*: You will find yourself a burned out, cynical, bitter individual who missed out on all the rewards of teaching and touching lives.

The choice seems obvious, but remember, the main difference between truly effective and truly ineffective teachers lies in the choices they have made along the way. Make the "right" choice!

"As a mother of three children and an active participant in their educations, I have had several conferences with teachers over the years. It's important to me to feel free to voice my concerns. I have always respected those teachers who were genuinely interested in my children as "people" and were willing to work cooperatively with me in solving problems. That makes a big difference to a parent. I'm much more likely to support a teacher who will listen to my concerns and not just dismiss me as an overbearing parent. I want only the best for my children, and I want for every one of their teachers to want that also."

Jennica Angelette, Parent

Learn to Work Cooperatively with Parents

As I walked down the hall of a high school one day, I met up with a brand-new, first-time teacher. She was in tears. I asked her what was wrong, and she answered, "I'm on my way to call a parent who's really upset with me, and I don't know how to defend myself against her." "Why is she upset with you?" I asked. "Well, we sent out letters to all of our homeroom students' parents and invited them to come in for private conferences. This parent claims she never got the letter, but I know I mailed all of them." "Okay," I said, "I'm going to walk you through this. First of all, let's capitalize on the very positive fact that this parent cares enough about her child's education to want to come to a conference." "I never thought about it that way," said the new teacher. I then told her exactly what to say during the phone conversation. Here are the instructions I gave her.

- Begin by saying, "I understand that you're very upset about not receiving a letter regarding the parent conferences. And I just want you to know that I was very impressed with the fact that you cared enough about your son to want to come to school and meet with his teacher. That says a lot about you as a parent."

- Then say, "I'm so sorry that you didn't receive the letter. But I'm anxious to meet with you, and I'm willing to do my best to accommodate your schedule."

- Next, ask, "What would be a convenient time for us to meet?"

Professionalism: Attitudes and Behaviors of Effective Teachers ◆ 79

Notice that nothing in the above conversation was in any way defensive. That's important, because when parents are angry, teachers often make the mistake of engaging in the struggle and arguing with them. What they should really do is allow parents to express their concerns, remaining calm and professional throughout. You see, when a person is angry, the anger can only last so long, unless, of course, the other party is fueling it. If the other party remains calm and does not get defensive, the angry parent will soon run out of steam. That's the opportunity to begin solving the problem.

Anyway, the new teacher went into the office to use the phone and I waited out in the hall. About five minutes later, she walked out of the office beaming. She said to me, "We're best friends now! She and I really hit it off after I complimented her on her genuine concern for her son. We're meeting tomorrow."

Yes, it really can be that simple. Approach all parents with the assumption that they truly do want what's best for their children, and work cooperatively and professionally with them in helping to achieve a common goal. Listen to them when they are upset, let them blow off steam if necessary, and then establish the fact that you're anxious to work cooperatively with them to solve the problem. Also, try to ensure that your comments include their child's strengths. Make it a practice to establish positive communication with parents up front, and then, when the occasional negative situation occurs, they will be much more willing to work cooperatively with *you* in solving the problem. Parents are much more likely to support you when they believe that you are genuinely interested in their child. And even if a parent walks out of a conference disagreeing with you, make sure that he or she walks out knowing that you acted professionally and did not lose your cool. You might not be able to control all of an angry parent's reactions, but you can most certainly control your own reactions in every such situation.

> ### Who's to Blame?
>
> *The college professor said*, "Such rawness in a student is a shame. Lack of preparation in high school is to blame."
>
> *Said the high school teacher*, "Good heavens, that boy's a fool. The fault, of course, is with the middle school."
>
> *The middle school teacher said*, "From stupidity may I be spared. They sent him in so unprepared."
>
> *The primary teacher huffed*, "Kindergarten blockheads all. They call that preparation? Why, it's worse than none at all."
>
> *The kindergarten teacher said*, "Such lack of training never did I see. What kind of woman must that mother be?"
>
> *The mother said*, "Poor helpless child. He's not to blame. His father's people were all the same."
>
> *Said the father at the end of the line*, "I doubt the rascal's even mine."
>
> Anonymous

Tip 51

Steer Clear of the Blame Game

If you have been teaching for two weeks or more, then you can relate to "Who's to Blame?" If you have ever been a child, and I sincerely hope you have, then you can relate to "Who's to Blame?" Any parent can relate to "Who's to Blame?" We can all relate! Why? Because we've all been guilty of it from time to time. But the simple fact is that playing the blame game does us no good. It does not move us forward, it does not help children, it does not improve teaching, and it wastes our valuable time and energy.

Bottom line: In our classrooms, every year, we receive a certain group of students to teach. We do not get to "pick" them. We do not get to pick their parents. We do not have any say in their educational experiences prior to our teaching them. We do, however, get to take them as they are and help them to grow from there. If we are committed to doing that, then we have no time for blaming. We have only time, and not nearly enough of it, to teach each and every one of them, to share our gifts, to recognize theirs, and to help them become what they are capable of becoming.

> "I make a concerted effort to participate in school functions
> —ball games, band concerts, dances, drama functions, par-
> ent meetings, etc. It helps me to get to know both the stu-
> dents and their parents better. I believe it also sends a mes-
> sage to students and parents that I'm 'human' and that my
> students mean more to me than the academics I teach."
>
> Simone Labat,
> Middle-School Teacher

Participate in School Functions

Yes, we all have lives of our own outside of our teaching careers. If you're a new teacher, then you're the exception. (Just kidding—but I know it feels like you don't have a life outside of school right now!) Whenever possible, however, it is important that we participate in after-school functions. I'll share a real-life experience here. When I was in third grade, my sisters, a couple of friends, and I invited my third-grade teacher, Mrs. Robichaux, to a talent show that we were planning. Little did we ever dream that she would actually attend. In fact, we were so convinced that she wouldn't come that we never even got around to planning the talent show. But guess what? She showed up! We went into a panic, because we had nothing planned. We quickly hung a sheet on the clothesline—our curtain—seated Mrs. Robichaux in a chair, and huddled behind the curtain to come up with something, anything! We were desperate. Thank goodness that my younger sister, Andrée, loved to perform. We kept sending her out to entertain Mrs. Robichaux. She first sang, "Leaving on a Jet Plane." Mrs. Robichaux clapped enthusiastically, and Andrée returned to us behind the curtain. We then sent her out to exhibit her gymnastic abilities. The poor little thing, only 6 years old at the time, was exhausted. But each time we sent her out, Mrs. Robichaux acted as though it was the most amazing talent she had ever witnessed. Then we all came out, took a bow, and Mrs. Robichaux left. In retrospect, I'm sure that Mrs. Robichaux knew, after the first act, that we had nothing prepared. But she never let on. She never even commented on the fact that the only participant in the entire talent show was my little sister. The following day, she thanked us for inviting her and said how much she had enjoyed herself. And we realized how much Mrs. Robichaux really cared. She gave of her own time, after school hours, to come and watch a six-year-old turn cartwheels across the yard. Is that dedication or what?

Participation in school functions sends a message to students and to parents that you care. No, our mother was not happy with us when she learned of what we had put poor Mrs. Robichaux through. However, she was definitely impressed with the fact that Mrs. Robichaux had not only endured, but pretended to enjoy, our "talent" show. Parents who believe that you care about their children will be much more likely to support you and work cooperatively with you. Students who believe that you care about them will work harder, will behave better, and will even "turn cartwheels" for you! As the saying goes, "Students won't care how much you know until they know how much you care."

P. S. Andrée went on to receive a Master's Degree in the Performing Arts. We think that Mrs. Robichaux's unbridled enthusiasm and encouragement had something to do with it!

> **"Anyone who stops learning is old, whether at twenty or at eighty."**
>
> Henry Ford

Resist the Temptation for More "Stuff"

Researchers tell us that the effects of an ineffective teacher can be seen in student test scores years down the road. To some, that research seems amazing. Isn't it funny, however, that we do not need research to tell us that the effects of an ineffective surgeon can be seen in patient x-rays years down the road? That's just common sense! Question: If patients are dying on a particular surgeon's operating table, do we simply buy the surgeon a new scalpel, a new video series, or, better yet, spruce up the operating room? Can you see where I'm going with this? Why is it that when students are not achieving in our classrooms, we tend to buy more "stuff," implement more programs, or, better yet, spruce up the physical surroundings?

To prove this point, put yourself in the position of a parent who has a choice between two schools for his child. Would you choose a school with little resources, few programs, but all effective teachers, or would you choose a school with lots of money, every program imaginable, but all ineffective teachers? As a new teacher, in which of the above two schools would you choose to teach? As an administrator, in which school would you want to work? The fact is that I have yet to meet a parent, a teacher, or an administrator who would opt for the school with ineffective teachers. As teachers, we don't need more "stuff." What we need are good models, supportive surroundings, and a desire to continue to improve our teaching skills. Remember, no amount of stuff will make us better teachers. And even the most effective of educational programs will fall flat in the hands of an ineffective teacher. Just as the scalpel is only as good as the surgeon, a teaching tool is only as good as the teacher using it. Ineffective teachers focus on hoarding "stuff." Effective teachers focus on honing skills!

"By swallowing evil words unsaid, no one has ever yet harmed his stomach."

Winston Churchill

Avoid Lounge Gossip

The old adage, "Anyone who will gossip with you will gossip about you" is true. And if you stop to think about it, speaking ill of others serves only to harm. No one has ever earned the respect of others by gossiping. And many are the cases of students being treated unfairly by teachers because these teachers had been "warned" and unjustly "biased" before even meeting the students. I've always thought that one of the many pluses for both teachers and students is the fact that we have the wonderful advantage of being able to start all over every single year. Imagine if you, as a teacher, would continue to be judged and evaluated by your administrator on previous mistakes you have made in your teaching or in your life, for that matter. That would be ludicrous. Many of us would be doomed before we even began a new year. And sadly, many students are "doomed" each year because of the careless, harmful words spoken about them between teachers. If you are a teacher, you will encounter others, somewhere along the way, who will try to engage with you in empty, meaningless gossip. Do not participate. Not only is it unprofessional, but it symbolizes the antithesis of what we truly stand for—serving and helping others. If you can't say something nice about someone, don't say anything.

Tip 54

> "Whenever I feel like I can't handle the demands of my job, when everything seems to be overwhelming, when I wonder if I'm really making a difference, I always stop and remind myself why I chose this profession in the first place. My focus goes back to what really matters—the children—and I realize that I *am* making a contribution, that I *am* touching lives."
>
> Francis Rodriguez,
> Curriculum Supervisor

Remind Yourself Why You Chose to Become a Teacher

Okay, so we all entered the profession of teaching for the same reason—the money! (Ha!) Seriously, I believe that, as teachers, we all share a common bond and a common purpose. In my trainings with teachers, I often begin by having them state why they entered the profession. It is always inspirational to hear the same thing, yet stated in unique ways by each teacher. The prevailing theme? "I wanted to make a difference, to touch lives." And it never fails. Following the training session, someone always comes up to me and says, "Thanks for helping me to remember why I became a teacher. I had almost forgotten."

In the everyday mayhem of our lives, we often get "caught up" in the negatives. It can happen in our personal lives, and it can happen in our professional lives. In teaching, it is sometimes all too easy to lose sight of our main focus, our students. I once had a meeting with a teacher who just needed to "vent." The conversation went like this: "I can't understand why we've adopted yet another new program. The pendulum just keeps swinging back and forth. I'm up to my ears in paperwork, and I've just been asked to chair yet another committee. The whole educational system seems to be going down like a sinking ship. When are we going to get a break? Why don't they just leave us alone?" The conversation continued, all in the same tone. After listening to her express her frustrations, I asked, "Tell me what brought you here. What made you choose this profession?" The teacher went on to share a touching story about a teacher who had influenced her life in so many ways. She said, "Realizing what a difference she made with me, one student of many, I decided that that's what I wanted to do—to make a difference in the lives of children, just as my teacher had done for me." I didn't have to say another word. The teacher smiled warmly and said, "Thanks for reminding me of that. I guess I was losing sight of the only thing that really matters in this profession—making a difference."

Yes, teaching is stressful and at times overwhelming. When you feel like you're at the end of your rope, remind yourself that *you* are a rope—a lifeline for the students that you teach. It won't lessen the workload, but it surely will make it seem much more bearable!

"He who is afraid of asking is afraid of learning."

Danish Proverb

Ask for Assistance

This tip goes hand in hand with Tip 61 (Ask Lots of Questions). However, whereas Tip 61 focuses on asking questions when you do not know something, here, the focus is on asking others to provide assistance to you. These "others" could include administrators, mentor teachers, fellow teachers, students, parents, and community members.

As a teacher said to me recently, "I'm not a one-man show. I enlist the support of anyone who can provide assistance in helping my students to learn." This was a high-school teacher who had his students assist him in decorating the room, gathering materials for activities, and just about anything else with which he needed help. He often had community members serving as guest speakers in his classroom. A group of volunteer parents were regularly in his classroom assisting with a multitude of tasks. And he even had other teachers coming in to demonstrate techniques for the benefit of both him and his students. He was a mentor to a new teacher, and he claimed that he got more innovative ideas from the new teacher than from any other member on the staff. "I believe in teamwork," he said. "When you get everyone involved, not only does it keep your classroom interesting, but it lets parents feel like active participants in their children's education. It also allows the community to get involved, which is beneficial to all." His science projects were always the "hit" of the year, and he invited everyone to attend. "Anyone is welcomed in our classroom. But I'm warning you that if you walk in, we'll put you to work."

Not only was this teacher willing to ask for assistance in the education of his students, but the students also went out into the community to volunteer their time and efforts in providing assistance to others. "It's a reciprocal kind of thing," he said. "We like to accept assistance from others, and we like to give something back. I think the most surprising thing to many is that so many people out there—colleagues, administrators, parents, community members, etc.—are so willing to provide assistance. All you have to do is ask!"

> **"When we do the best we can, we never know what miracle is wrought in our life, or in the life of another."**
>
> Helen Keller

Be the Best You Can Be

There is little in life that gives us more satisfaction than knowing that we have done something and given it our best. Teaching gives us that opportunity every single day. No teacher is perfect. All teachers make mistakes. But teachers who give their best every single day are the ones who touch lives. In teaching, even the most difficult days can be successful ones when we are resolved to give it our all. In fact, the most difficult days are often the most rewarding ones—those days when we are truly put to the test. There will be days when you are not feeling well, either emotionally or physically, but if you choose to come to school, you must teach at your best. There will be days when students try your patience because they do not understand what you're trying to teach. Again, try a new way of explaining it, and do not give in to frustration. Do not give up, and do not give in. Rather, give it all you've got—and then some.

It is only in giving our best that we can possibly expect to bring out the best in our students. And in doing our best, we never know "what miracle is wrought...in the life of another." So be the best teacher you can be, and your rewards will come to you in the form of young hearts and young lives forever changed because of your influence.

> ## Which Way?
>
> *I stood at a fork in the road*
> *And didn't know which way to go*
> *But since I had no destination in mind*
> *If I got there, I'd never know!*
>
> Annette L. Breaux,
> *No Adults Allowed*

Set Goals for Your Own Improvement

Most people have goals, lots of them. But many never accomplish them. Think about your own New Year's resolutions. We all make them. "I'm going to get skinny." "I'm going to save more money." "I'm going to get rid of the clutter in my house." "I'm going to be a nicer person." Notice how vague these goals are. There's no real plan of action, so they usually don't get accomplished. It would be far more "doable" to say, "I'm going to walk 20 minutes a day, three days a week." "I'm going to increase my monthly contributions to my savings by 5 percent." "I'm going to have a garage sale to get rid of things around the house that I don't need." "I'm going to make a concerted effort to do something nice for someone, just one thing, every day." And then you write them down and keep them in a place where you will see them daily. Goals are accomplished one step at a time. And written goals are far more likely to be accomplished than those we just "store" in our heads.

In the classroom, you might say, "I'm going to learn to implement cooperative learning this year." "I'm going to devise a new classroom management plan and implement it consistently." "I'm going to write activities into my lesson plans, daily, that are student-oriented."

Whatever your goals are, write them and post them. Take one step toward your goals every day, and you're sure to get there. Don't just stand at the fork in the road scratching your head. Get the end in mind first, map out your plan, and drive toward your destination without taking any detours. Do stop, of course, for fuel, food, and bathrooms!

> "In training teachers, I often tell them the following: 'Blessed are the flexible, for they shall not be bent out of shape.' We always get a good laugh out of it, but the truth is that it really does happen. I've seen teachers literally look 'bent out of shape.' In this business, you have got to be flexible if you're going to be successful."
>
> Barbara Thibodaux,
> Teacher Trainer and Consultant

Be Flexible

Any teacher will tell you that in teaching there are both predictabilities and unpredictabilities. Here are some of the unpredictabilities:

- Fire drills
- Unexpected intercom announcements
- Children getting sick
- Unexpected discipline challenges
- Unanticipated student questions
- Schedule changes
- Knocks at the classroom door
- Unannounced observations by administration
- Running out of time to teach a particular skill
- Overestimating the time it will take to teach a particular skill
- Policy changes
- Changes in teaching assignments, and so on and so on and so on....

As a new teacher shared with me, "The only real predictability about teaching is the fact that it is unpredictable." She went on to explain that during her very first month of teaching, she seriously considered resigning. "I like things to go just as I plan," she said. "Here I was with my lessons perfectly planned, thinking that no one and nothing would interrupt my teaching. Boy, was I wrong! I soon learned to get over it and to go with the flow. Now, when someone knocks at my door unexpectedly or when there are sudden schedule changes or candy sales or fire drills or whatever, I don't let myself get so upset." This new teacher was absolutely correct in saying that the only predictability in teaching is that it is unpredictable! Get accustomed to it,

Tip 59

and learn to roll with the punches. Don't let yourself get bent out of shape by things over which you have no control. Be flexible. If you don't learn to bend, you're going to eventually break!

> **"A man should never be ashamed to own he has been in the wrong, which is but saying, in other words, that he is wiser today than he was yesterday."**
>
> Jonathon Swift

Learn and Grow from Your Mistakes

In Tip 29, we discuss how to recover quickly when making mistakes. In Tip 100, we discuss teaching students that mistakes are wonderful learning opportunities. In this tip, we focus on learning and growing from our own mistakes—practicing what we preach to our students. Mistakes are everywhere. We all make them, and we make them often. They are always a means to learning and growing, if we allow them to be.

It was my first year of teaching. All of my students were eagerly awaiting the "trial run" for the science fair. I set a table in the front of the classroom, and my students began, one by one, to display and explain their projects. One student's project involved helium. He was going to demonstrate, with an actual model, how a hot air balloon works. I sat anxiously in the back of the room waiting to see the magic. Right as he was about to light the match, one of the other students looked at me and asked, "Don't you think we'd better go outside for this experiment, since it involves fire?" How could I have been so stupid? I quickly agreed, and we took the experiment outside. Sure enough, something went wrong with the experiment, and the balloon burst into flames. What a close call! My dear, sweet students never said a word, but I'm sure they knew how I was feeling—extremely relieved, yet extremely dimwitted. When we returned to the room, I thanked them for their excellent display of common sense, and I learned a very important lesson about thinking in advance and using common sense.

Every mistake we make is an invitation to learn and an opportunity to grow. You will make lots of them in your teaching. Just make sure that you put them to good use!

Tip 60

Tip 61

> ## Too Many Questions
>
> *You say I ask too many questions*
> *But you just don't seem to see*
> *That I wonder about so many things*
> *For which answers there surely must be*
> *But once I know an answer*
> *A new question grows in my mind*
> *Because what I learn uncovers*
> *New problems with answers to find*
> *So be patient with my questioning*
> *There still is so much I don't know*
> *But I do know that learning more answers*
> *Will certainly help me to grow.*
>
> Annette L. Breaux,
> *No Adults Allowed*

Ask Lots of Questions

A struggling new teacher shared the following with me: "I have so many questions, but I don't know whom to ask. I'm afraid to look 'stupid,' so I can't ask other teachers. They'll probably think to themselves, 'If she's a teacher, then she should know these things.' Then my reputation will suffer."

Sadly, this is a very typical concern of new teachers. They're afraid to ask, for fear of appearing incompetent. This is what they do not yet know:

- ◆ Teaching is not an exact science, so all teachers should remain in a state of questioning.

- ◆ Teachers, in general, are more than willing to share, with new teachers and veteran teachers, their techniques, their ideas, their philosophies, what works for them, and what has *not* worked for them.

- ◆ Asking questions does not make you look incompetent. Rather, it makes you look like a dedicated professional who wants to do what's best for students.

- ◆ True professionals will not sacrifice learning something new for fear of appearing ignorant. We are all ignorant when it comes to teaching. There's so much we don't yet know.

Simply put, any teacher, regardless of years of experience, who does not ask questions will stagnate. So ask lots of questions. Just be prepared for the fact that every time you get one question answered, it will open a whole new world of possibilities, for which you'll have more questions, which will, of course, lead to more answers which will then awaken new questions which will require more answers.

Any questions?

"The biggest mistake I made as a new teacher was trying to dress like the students. I was all of 22 years old, and I was teaching high school seniors. I though they would think I was 'cool' if I dressed the way they did. They thought I was 'cool' all right, but they didn't respect me as a teacher."

Beth C., Teacher

Dress Like a Professional

In your mind's eye, imagine an attorney, male or female, defending a case in the courtroom. How is he/she dressed? Chances are that you are visualizing a man in a coat and tie or a woman in a business suit. Now do the same thing, this time imagining a professional businessman or businesswoman. Once again, chances are good that you have a clear image of a person dressed very professionally. Okay, now imagine a teacher, male or female. Isn't it true that no "clear" image comes to mind? I conduct this activity with teachers across the country, and without fail, they always admit that they have a much more difficult time conjuring up a clear image of how a teacher "looks." And for those who do manage to see an image, they readily admit that the teacher does not look as professional as the attorney or the businessperson. Why is this? And is it important? Well, whether we like it or not, people do tend to judge us by our appearances. Others will more readily treat a professionally dressed person in a professional manner. That's a fact. And it applies to the classroom. Students, parents, and coworkers automatically treat teachers who dress professionally with more respect. That is not to say, of course, that "looking the part" is all there is to earning respect. You also have to "act the part."

In inducting our new teachers every year, we play a "trick" on them. Here's how it works. We introduce the induction team, one of whom is a principal. The other three induction team members are all dressed very professionally, but the principal is not. She wears a tee shirt, blue jeans, and tennis shoes. The new teachers don't say anything, but it's always funny to see the looks on their faces. This is a principal? This is one of our presenters? She's going to be teaching us how to teach?

We don't say a word. We simply introduce her, she welcomes everyone, and then she leaves. Later during the day, right before her first presentation, she remains out of the room. I ask the new teachers, "What was wrong when I introduced Ms. Brooks to you this morning? You seemed a little shocked about something." It never fails. They always tell me that they were surprised by the way she was dressed. "Well, what was wrong with the way she was dressed? Was she indecent?" I ask. "No," they answer. "But she just didn't look like a professional should look," they add. "Well," I say, "would you be more comfortable if she came in looking like this?" She now walks in, dressed professionally, and two things happen: a) They know they've been tricked, and b) They realize that, without our "preaching" to them, we have made a very important statement about how we, as a school district, value professional attire.

Teachers are professionals. They should "look" like professionals. And dressing professionally does not mean being uncomfortable. It also does not mean buying expensive clothing. It simply means looking "different" from the students. Remember, you are a teacher. Dress the part, act the part, and you will be treated as you so deserve—like a true professional!

Who better to judge our effectiveness than our students?

Devise a "Teacher Report Card"

During my third year of teaching, I read, in a magazine for teachers, about the idea of a "teacher report card." I thought to myself: My students receive report cards every nine weeks, yet they never get the opportunity to evaluate me, to tell me how *I'm* doing as their teacher. I loved the idea, though I must admit that it was a bit frightening, knowing that my students would be brutally honest with me, but then again, who better to judge my effectiveness than my own students? They were my "clients." I was there to serve them. Why shouldn't they be allowed to provide me with feedback as to how I was doing? I implemented the idea immediately, and the students loved it. They were a little amazed at the fact that they were actually going to "grade" their teacher.

The report card was simple and to the point. It had no space for the student's name, because the best way to get honest feedback from students is to allow them to express themselves anonymously. Items included were:

- ♦ Does my teacher make class interesting? If not, what could she do to make the class more interesting?
- ♦ Does my teacher care about me as a person?
- ♦ Does my teacher hold me accountable for my actions?
- ♦ Am I allowed to contribute my opinions in this class?
- ♦ Does my teacher treat all students fairly and with dignity and respect?
- ♦ Am I successful in this class? If not, what could my teacher do to help me to become more successful?
- ♦ Does my teacher enjoy teaching?
- ♦ Do I feel that my teacher is the best teacher she can be?
- ♦ What I like about this class is _____.
- ♦ What I do not like about this class is _____.
- ♦ If I could change one thing about this class, it would be _____.

Each nine weeks, when my students received their report cards, I also received mine. And I can tell you that it was the most useful and honest feedback that I ever received in my teaching.

Allowing your students to "grade" your performance accomplishes several things:

- It holds you, as their teacher, accountable.
- It gives a message to students that their opinions matter.
- It shows students that their input is valued.
- It keeps you on your toes!

Devise your own teacher report card, and allow your students to provide you with useful, honest, and valuable feedback. They will!

> **"Children have never been very good at listening to their elders, but they have never failed to imitate them."**
>
> James Baldwin

Be a Role Model for Your Students

When we sign a contract and call ourselves "teacher," we have accepted the profound responsibility of being a role model to every one of our students. Students need role models, and they seek them out in their lives. Think back to your own role models. We all had them. They were the people who cared about you, who encouraged your success, who inspired you to accomplish. They were people who possessed qualities that you wanted to emulate. I often tell teachers that their students watch them very closely, and that their actions, of course, speak much louder than their words. As teachers, we often forget just how loudly our actions speak, and we end up modeling the exact opposites of the lessons we're trying to teach our students. It looks something like this:

Teacher yells at a student—"Don't you yell at me, young lady!"

Teacher, with a very unpleasant look, says to a belligerent student— "Take that look off of your face!"

These are actual scenarios of actual teachers modeling the exact behaviors they were trying to prevent in students! You see, students notice everything. Isn't it true that they notice when you wear a new outfit? Isn't it true that they notice when you get a haircut? Isn't it true that they notice when you are not feeling well? And isn't it true that they notice if you treat one student in a more favorable way than other students?

To further prove the point, just in case you are not convinced of how closely your students watch your actions, here is a challenge for you. I challenge you to walk into your classroom tomorrow and ask, "Would any of you like to imitate me?" Guess what? They'll imitate you, and they'll do it well!

Remember: Students may not always do what you say, but they are sure to imitate what you do! Make sure that what you "do" is to act as a positive role model for all of them.

In the words of Albert Schweitzer, *"Example is not the best way to influence people; it is the only way."*

> **"Self-control is the hardest victory."**
>
> Aristotle

Self-Control

Someone made me mad today
and I'm wanting to unload
My temperature is boiling hot
and I feel like I'll explode
My face is really red right now
and my veins are sticking out
I bet I would feel better
if I'd kick and scream and shout
But I'm thinking if I did that
I'd look as bad as they
And I'm sure that I'd regret it
if I said what I'd like to say
So I'm trying to calm myself right now
I'm giving it all I've got
Cause if I maintain self-control
I will have gained A LOT!

Annette L. Breaux,
No Adults Allowed

Tip 65

Maintain Your Composure

It's not our feelings that determine who we are to others, but rather our actions. And one of the most difficult tasks to accomplish as a teacher is the ability to control your actions and maintain your composure at all costs. Yes, students will "try" you. They will "work on your nerves." They will "go for your jugular"—not because they're bad, but because they're children. And to be able to "control" an adult's emotions is a very powerful feeling for a child. An important word of advice: Don't play the game. You will feel frustrated at times. That's normal. But to roll your eyes, clench your teeth when you speak, fold your arms and tap your foot as you stare at the ceiling, sigh, raise your voice, or exhibit any of the many signs of a loss of composure will only serve to let students know that you *did* play, you *did* lose, and you gave your control over to them. You can be serious without looking angry. You can discipline a child in a thoughtful, professional manner. You see, there is never an appropriate time to "lose your cool." You are a professional, and you must act as a professional at all times. Therefore, you must "never let them see you sweat." When students realize that you will not play the game and that you are truly a professional, they will stop trying to see how red they can make your face get, how far that vein in your neck will stick out.... You will, in turn, earn their respect, but most importantly, you will serve as the role model that so many of them so desperately need.

"In 2001, I was promoted to a middle-school principalship. I consider myself fortunate to have inherited a faculty that was hungry for leadership. Even though they did not always agree with some of my policies, they were professional and supportive enough to enforce them. They soon began to realize that these new policies resulted in a more positive school climate. Teamwork is so important to the success of a school. It requires mutual respect between administrators and teachers."

Linda Nance, Principal

Cooperate with Administration

I often hear teachers complaining about their administrators. I typically listen for a while and then ask, "What percentage of the school day do you typically spend in your classroom with your students?" The answer is usually about 90 percent. Then I ask, "What percentage of the day do you spend in the presence of your administrator?" The answer is usually 1 percent or less, unless, of course, the teacher is married to his or her administrator, and since I'm not a marriage counselor, I leave immediately! The fact remains that some teachers spend a good percentage of the time complaining about someone they hardly see. Wouldn't it make more sense to put 100 percent of your efforts into the people with whom you spend more than 90 percent of your school day?

It will never happen that all of the teachers will agree with administrative decisions all of the time. If you feel strongly about a particular issue, then you should discuss it privately and professionally with your administrator. But if the issue is one over which you have no control, then let it go. I once knew a teacher who spent a considerable amount of her time griping about the dress code. She wanted to wear blue jeans, and the policy forbade it. She allowed that one issue to consume her. In anger, she turned against the administrator and refused to support any of his decisions. This, of course, was unprofessional. It affected her entire personality, so the students suffered also.

In a truly effective school, teachers work together in cooperation with administration. They don't always agree with administration, yet they support administrative decisions, as much as possible, for the betterment of the school and ultimately the students. Don't get caught up in petty issues that lead to breakdowns in communication and cooperation. Remember, as discussed in Tip 69, to focus on what you *can* change—not on what you *can't*. When we focus our efforts on working cooperatively toward a common goal—helping children—we may not always agree, but our students will always benefit.

> "Speak when you are angry, and you will make the best speech you will ever regret."

> Ambrose Bierce

Avoid "Acting When Angry"

We've all been there. We can remember the feeling of boiling blood pulsing through our veins, building and building, racing through our bodies, and then—*bang*—an explosion! We got angry, and we lost control. We said things that, to this day, regardless of how long ago it happened, we still regret. How we wish we could take it all back. Well, we can't. And the bad news is that we've probably all been guilty of not learning a lesson from it. We get angry again, and we act or speak without thinking. Once again, we lament the fact that we allowed ourselves to give in to the anger. We are all human. We all have emotions. We all experience anger. But not everyone expresses his anger in the same way. Feelings don't determine how others perceive us, but our actions surely do.

A teacher stood in front of her classroom and "warned" her students several times to stop talking. They would stop for a few minutes, and then the talking would resume. Because I was seated in the back of the room, I literally watched her getting angrier with each warning. Her face became redder, her breathing became labored, her body became tense, and, finally, she exploded. She threw her book down and began screaming at the students. She then went into a tirade that she later regretted. But she couldn't take it back.

We often hear it suggested that when angry, we should "count to 10" or do something to calm ourselves in order to avoid saying or doing something we'll later regret. Anger is a very powerful emotion. And in the classroom, it can be a very dangerous emotion if we do not control it. Just as we try to teach students to recognize their anger for what it is and to avoid losing control of themselves, so must we, as their teachers and role models, model appropriate ways of dealing with situations that cause us to feel anger. It is never appropriate to lose control of your emotions in the classroom. When you're so angry that you can't think straight, you're right—you can't think straight. Wait until you can, and think about how you will handle the situation from a logical perspective.

FACT: If you do not have personal problems, then you are not a person. However, if you allow your personal problems to spill over into your classroom, then you are not a professional!

Do Not Allow Your Personal Problems to Spill Over into the Classroom

Yes, we all have lives outside of teaching, and we all struggle with our own trials and tribulations. That's normal. What is not normal is to allow those struggles to affect our students. I once heard a teacher announce to her class, "Look, I'm having a bad day. I've been up all night with a sick child, so I'm warning you that I'm not in a good mood. I'm going to try to concentrate on my teaching, but I'm tired. Also, we've fallen way behind in the textbook, so we're going to have to move fast today. So stay in your seats, and don't mess with me!"

Okay, now imagine an airline pilot in a similar situation. The "welcome" announcement would sound something like this: "Good morning ladies and gentlemen. This is your pilot speaking, and boy, am I having a bad day! I've been up all night with a sick child, so I'm not in a good mood. I'm going to try to get you to New York, but I'm tired, so I am not promising you anything. Also, we've fallen way behind on our flights, so we're going to have to fly extra fast! So stay in your seats, and don't mess with me!"

What would you do as a passenger on this plane? You'd get off, immediately, even in midflight! The fact is that students don't have the luxury of getting out of your classroom. However, they would feel the same way, in your classroom, that you would feel on that flight.

I'm sure that somewhere out there, there are pilots who are not having the best days of their lives. The trick is not to let their bad days affect their passengers. And so it should be in the classroom. Students are not vents for our frustrations. If you're having a day that is so bad that you feel you cannot teach, then stay home. If you choose to come to school however, be a professional! All "passengers" in your classroom should enjoy a safe flight and an on-time arrival.

> **"Make the best use of what is in your power, and take the rest as it happens."**
>
> Epictetus

Focus on What You *Can* Change

Okay, so your administrator does not always see things the way you see them. Maybe Zagat's will never rate the food in the school cafeteria. The school custodian may miss a spot or two on occasion, and parents may not rear their children in ways that meet your standards. But what does that have to do with what goes on within the four walls of your classroom? Very little, if anything. The fact is that many people spend 90 percent of their time focusing on things they simply cannot change. As teachers, we must learn to place 100 percent of our energies on things we can do something about. And we can absolutely do something about the teaching and learning that takes place in our classrooms, every single day of the school year. The following are examples of teachers focusing needless energy on things they can do very little about:

♦ "I met Brandon's parents yesterday, and now I understand why he's like he is. He doesn't stand a chance."

♦ "Why is it that our principal won't allow us to go on a field trip?"

♦ "Did you hear what Mrs. _____ told her students today?"

♦ "How can they expect us to teach from this textbook?"

♦ "Have you noticed the way that Mr. _____ looks at Ms. _____? I think there's something going on."

♦ "Kids today are just not what they used to be."

♦ "How I wish I had my time in. I'd retire today."

All right, I think you get the point. A good rule of thumb is this: When faced with a problem at school, ask yourself, "Is there anything I can do to remedy this situation? If so, what's my plan of action?" If your answer is no, then let it go. If your answer is yes, then *do* something! Yes, the faculty lounge might become a dull place, but you'll be so busy working on solutions to *real* problems that you won't have time to spend there anyway!

"Never become so much of an expert that you stop gaining expertise. View life as a continuous learning experience."

Denis Waitley

Grow as a Professional

Whether you have been teaching one year or 31 years, you should be in a constant state of improving. I've often heard it said that some people teach 30 years, and some people teach one year 30 times! Education is like the field of medicine. We are constantly learning new and better ways of doing things.

A superintendent recently told me that he requires *all* of his 2000 teachers to write professional growth plans, every year. These plans include the teachers' yearly goals for improvement. The plans are monitored on an ongoing basis and are then evaluated at the end of the year. "This ensures that *all* of my teachers are constantly getting better," he said. "We don't expect perfection, but we insist on improvement." When asked about why the goals were written and evaluated, he said, "It's a fact that people who have specific written goals are far more successful than those who have vague mental goals. That's why we also have district-wide goals, and they're posted in every single classroom. We have a definite direction, and everyone is headed that way." Upon asking a teacher in this district about her professional growth plan, she responded, "I wasn't crazy about the idea at first. It seemed like just one more thing we had to do, and I already had plenty enough to do. But having these goals keeps me sharp. I set them, and then I move toward them. And I always arrive at my destination a much more competent teacher." In the words of John Cotton Dana, "Who dares to teach must never cease to learn."

For more on goal setting, see Tip 58.

Tip 70

Motivation
and Rapport

> ### I'm Not My Older Brother
>
> *I'm not my older brother*
> *So please do not compare*
> *To treat me as another*
> *Would surely be unfair*
> *He has ways of doing things*
> *Ways that are his own*
> *He's okay, but there's no way*
> *That I'll become his clone*
> *I'm not my older brother*
> *And I do not wish to be*
> *I'm happy to be who I am*
> *And that is simply me.*
>
> Annette L. Breaux,
> *No Adults Allowed*

Celebrate the Uniqueness of Your Students

Every student is his own person, a unique individual with unique talents, skills, strengths, and dreams. Yet, we often try to make our students something they're not. We compare them to their siblings or to other students. Ask any parent who has two or more children if any of their children are even remotely alike. The answer will be a resounding *no*. Our job, as teachers, is to find the unique aspects of every student we teach and to celebrate those qualities. I am not, of course, referring to a student's unique quality of being the most disruptive person in the classroom. Find the strengths and talents in each student, and nurture those.

A high-school student once told me, "The thing I like best about 'Mr. C' is that he doesn't compare me to my brothers. I'm the youngest of six boys, and they've all gone to this same school. So, every year, I'm known by most of my teachers as the last of the Patterson boys. We all look alike, so they expect that we all *are* alike, and we're not. I like my brothers, all right, but I don't want to walk in their footsteps. I've got my own path mapped out. Anyway, 'Mr. C' never even mentions my brothers, and he's taught them all. He just acts as if I'm a regular guy, my own person."

Remember that each student is a unique individual, his own person. Treat him that way. Celebrate who he is rather than pushing him to be something he's not.

To put it in its simplest terms: *I am me. I am not you. If you should think that I am you, please see me.*

> **"The teacher who is attempting to teach without inspiring the pupil with a desire to learn is hammering on cold iron."**
>
> Horace Mann

Light a Spark in Your Students

I cannot think of a more simplified way to stress the importance of lighting a spark in your students than by saying the following:

> What really matters is not so much what students walk away with in their "hands," but rather how many sparks were ignited in their "hearts." Students don't want more "stuff." They want "inspiration." And it takes talent to inspire. That's why it is the *teacher* who is the key to the success of the students in the classroom. The *teacher*, not the *content*, determines whether students walk away "ignited" or "extinguished."

I recently spoke to a seventh-grade student who had been retained three times. The student readily told me that he had never liked school because he just wasn't any good at it—that was, he said, until he encountered Mrs. Thomas, his seventh-grade teacher. From the very beginning of school, he felt inspired. He felt successful. He could hardly believe the feeling, as it was one he had never experienced in school. His grades soared, and he soon caught up with his classmates—so much so that the school decided to move him on to the ninth grade. The following is a quote from this student: "Being in Mrs. Thomas's class was like a dream come true. She made learning fun, and she found some talents in me that no one else had ever noticed. Had I had Mrs. Thomas years ago, I would probably be in the 'right' grade today. I'm not a failure. I guess I just needed to be inspired."

Would that we could all be Mrs. Thomases. And we can. Light a spark in every student you teach. Set them aglow with a desire to work harder, to search for answers, to acquire deeper understandings, to love learning, and to be better people. If you can do that, then you have done your job well.

Smile

If everyone smiled at everyone else
Who could ever get mad?
How long would it take for them to smile back?
And who could ever stay sad?
Surely the world would change, I think
With a smile on everyone's face
To think that simply a smile or a wink
Could make this a happier place.

Annette L. Breaux,
No Adults Allowed

Smile

A smile is, quite simply, the fastest way to get to a student's heart. Most of us know this, and most of us use it as often as possible. On the other side of that, however, there are a few veteran teachers out there who can't wait to give advice to new teachers. The advice is, "Whatever you do, don't smile until Christmas." Some poor unsuspecting teachers take this advice and quickly run into problems! Imagine sitting in a classroom all day where the teacher never smiles. Imagine refraining from smiling for even a day, much less until Christmas!

Smiles, by the way, are contagious. Try this experiment with your class. Simply stand in front of your class and smile—a really big smile with teeth showing! Don't say a word. Just smile, and watch what happens. They will, of course, begin smiling back at you. Yes, they will also wonder what's going on, but just to prove the point, try it. Some people smile more naturally than others. If you are not a natural "smiler," then do what I've seen many teachers do. Put a little note on your desk with a smiley face to remind you to make a concerted effort, every day, to smile as much as possible.

I tried an experiment with a new teacher one day. She was experiencing difficulty with student behavior. Upon observing her, I couldn't help but notice that she never smiled one time throughout the lesson. She looked like she was unhappy while she was teaching. So we agreed that for one solid day, she would teach with a pleasant demeanor and smile as often as possible. I gave her my home phone number and asked her to call me the following night to let me know of the results. The phone rang, and since smiles can literally be "heard" over the phone, I knew the experiment had worked. "They were so much better behaved today," she said. "And they even asked me what I was so happy about, which told me that I really needed to make the effort to smile more."

As an added benefit, medical research tells us that when we smile, we literally trick our brains into thinking that we are happy. This, in turn, releases endorphins that enhance our moods and boost our immune systems.

So here's to your health, your happiness, and your continued success in the classroom: Smile!

> "Aerodynamically, the bumble bee shouldn't be able to fly, but the bumble bee doesn't know it, so it goes on flying anyway."
>
> Mary Kay Ash

Give Your Students More Credit Than They Deserve

I sat at a teacher's desk one day during an observation. There, written on a note taped to her desk was the following: "My students might not be as good as I lead them to believe they are, but they'll try harder because of it." I couldn't wait to talk to her about this. When I asked her about it, she smiled and said, "That's my philosophy. I believe in giving my students just a little more credit than they deserve, and they always rise to the occasion. If they don't know they can't do something, then their chances of doing it are increased. I believe in helping students to believe in themselves, because once they believe in themselves, they're unstoppable!"

This teacher hit the nail on the head! Tell your students that they're a little better than they are, and they'll become a little better than they are. The key here is "a little." You do not want to tell a student who struggles to write a complete sentence that he is a brilliant writer. Use discretion and a little common sense.

There are lots of young bumble bees learning to fly in your classroom. Don't tell them they can't. Let them fly!

Tip 74

> "If you would win a man to your cause, first convince him that he is your friend."

Abraham Lincoln

Make Every Student Your "Favorite"

I often tell teachers that if I should walk into their classrooms and ask who the teacher's favorite student is, all hands should go up. And if a few hands remain down, I can practically guarantee that those are the students who tend to cause problems. Students who do not feel that you care are the ones most likely to seek your attention in inappropriate ways, as often as possible. The good news is that the opposite is also true. Once a student is convinced that you care about him, he will do almost anything to please you. He will act politely, he will do his work, he will behave appropriately, and he will even turn in homework! It's quite simple—students want to feel successful, appreciated, and respected. And though the task is no small one, you should make it a priority to somehow make each student feel that he is your "secret favorite." This can be accomplished by taking a personal interest in every student, by making sure that every student is experiencing success, and by doing all the little things that tell others we care about them. Show me a teacher who treats all students as "favorites," and I'll show you a classroom with no behavior problems and with high levels of student achievement!

> **"The man who can make hard things easy is the educator."**
>
> Ralph Waldo Emerson

Set the Stage for Success

It is true that nothing breeds success like success. Yet, many students do not experience much success in school. This does not have to be the case. Success does not look the same for all students, however, just as success does not look the same for any of us. If I could manage to change the oil in my car, it would be a tremendous success for me. To an auto mechanic, that would hardly be considered success. That's because success is relative. To be successful simply means to accomplish something, to achieve. Though all students may not be college bound, that definitely does not mean that they should not enjoy a multitude of successes in their schooling. In fact, successes in their schooling should help them in choosing a path to take for the future.

Nathan was fifteen years old and in the seventh grade. He arrived in my classroom announcing to me that he was there only because he had been expelled from his previous school and that he had no intentions of learning anything. He was simply biding his time until he could quit school. I knew I had to do something to make him successful, and the sooner the better! "By the way," he added, "you have a nice car." Bingo! He liked cars. I began to let him teach me everything he knew about cars, which was a lot. In class, I related every skill to a car or an engine in some kind of way. His writing and reading skills began to improve drastically, because we started from his level, which was quite low. But as much as possible, we wrote and read about cars. Soon, he was telling *me* how a particular skill reminded him of something having to do with cars or engines or motorcycles or you name it! Nathan was experiencing success and recognition possibly for the first time in his life. Not only did he remain in school that year, but he actually went on to receive a high school diploma. Some years later, I was filling my car at a local convenience store, and I heard a deep voice say, "How about a hug?" It was Nathan! He was now a very successful auto mechanic making a salary considerably higher than my own!

Okay, so Nathan was one wonderful success story, but how do you make *all* students successful? You meet them right where they are, and you move them forward from there. If you were to teach a group of students how to swim, would you begin in the deep water? Of course you wouldn't. You would begin in the shallow end of the pool. For some beginners, success might mean becoming comfortable with putting their feet in the water as they sit safely on the side of the pool. To other beginners, success might mean splashing around in the shallow water. Eventually, however, if you take them from where they are and nudge them gently forward, they will all learn to swim. Yes, some will become better swimmers than others. Some may simply learn to survive in the water, while others may become Olympians. But all will have experienced success. They will have achieved beyond their original levels of skill.

It is a fact that every student is successful at his own level. And every time he experiences just the tiniest taste of success, the satisfaction will spur him forward. So how do you make all students successful? You meet them right where they are, and you move them forward from there. Help your students to believe that they can, and they will!

> **"I can live for two months on a good compliment."**
>
> Mark Twain

Provide Positive Feedback

Research has concluded, time and again, that it takes several positive comments to neutralize one negative comment in the eyes of a student. However, in the typical school, the ratio of negative comments far outweighs the positive comments. We are all aware of the fact that positive environments are far more conducive to student cooperation and achievement than are negative environments. Yet many classrooms often resonate with the sounds of "Don't do that," "Stop it," "Be quiet," "Pay attention," "Sit up straight," "Go to the office," etc. The scenario is, regrettably, a little too familiar to us all.

In an attempt to see if it was possible to turn this situation around, I, along with one of my coworkers, decided to conduct an experiment. The experiment I'm about to share with you has produced amazingly positive results in every one of the 20-plus schools in which we've attempted it thus far. Here's how it works. I conduct a brief faculty in-service, sharing the information I have just shared with you regarding the typical ratio of positives to negatives in classrooms. Then I ask the faculty for permission to conduct an experiment with them, expressing my expectations that they will defy the research. They always agree to it. I tell them that my coworker and I will spend five minutes in each of their classrooms, and that we will simply be keeping a tally of positives and negatives. We will give credit for smiles, praise, constructive feedback to students, "positive" sayings on the walls, any type of positive comment made to students, etc. One stipulation is that students will not be made aware of what is going on. I also tell them the date that we will be conducting the experiment, and it never fails—every time, one or two teachers approach me afterward and say, "You shouldn't have told everyone the day you're coming. Some of them are very negative, and they'll just 'fake' being positive on the day that you're here." I always thank them for their concern and assure them that all will be fine. You see, I am intentionally setting them up for success, but they don't yet realize that.

On the day of the experiment, it is typical to identify a ratio of anywhere from 25 to 50 positive comments to every one negative. It is also very typical that on that day, student office referrals drop drastically. It's amazing! Teachers are smiling, students are smiling, and learning is evident. I then compile the results and return to speak to the faculty. I begin by congratulating them on their extremely positive school environment. I provide nothing but positive feedback, and they all beam with pride. They are always amazed at how well behaved the students were, especially because the students were not even aware of the experiment. And then, the real lesson: I share with them the fact that several of them seemed concerned that my announcing the date of the experiment would "sway" the results of the experiment. Then I say to them, "I have just taught you a very powerful lesson about teaching. I intentionally set you up for success. I told you the exact date of the experiment intentionally, knowing that you would make a concerted effort to be even more positive than you would normally be. You see, I didn't want to "catch" you doing something negative. Had I done that with a "surprise attack" experiment, the results may not have been quite as positive. Then, had I provided negative feedback, insisting that you change your attitudes, you would have become defensive and resentful. Instead, I set you up for success so that I could provide you with some useful, positive feedback. I simply wanted to prove to you that being positive makes a difference—a *big* difference. And remember, the only thing that was different was *your* attitude, *your* approach. The students had no idea what was going on, but they responded favorably to the positive environments in all of your classrooms."

"This," I tell them, "is how you want to approach your teaching. You want to set your students up for success by maintaining a positive attitude, providing positive feedback, and expressing belief in each student's abilities."

Oh, and something else that never fails—the assistant principals who usually handle the discipline referrals always ask me to come back tomorrow, and the next day, and the next!

A Very Clever Teacher

We had to draw a picture one day
But I couldn't decide what to draw
So I decided to leave my paper blank
And my teacher looked at it in awe
"What a beautiful fluffy white cloud," she said
"May I hang it on the wall?"
And I realized that she did not notice
That I had drawn nothing at all
Then she proudly hung for all to see
The work I had not done
But with her permission I took it home
And I added the sky and the sun
And now that I think about it
I wonder if she really knew
That my drawing was not of a cloud at all
It was work that I did not do
I thought that I had tricked her
But maybe it was she
Who used a clever way to get me to draw
A picture for all to see.

Annette L. Breaux,
No Adults Allowed

Tip 78

Use Clever Psychology

How many teachers truly utilize the kind of psychology that the teacher in the above poem uses? Many do, but many others do not. The "rule of thumb" is: You give an assignment, the child turns in a blank paper, and he gets an F. Not very conducive to improving student achievement! The fact is that with the right psychology, you can get a child to do just about anything. The most perfect example of this occurred recently. Liz Yates, a curriculum coordinator and former master teacher, went into a classroom to observe a new teacher. The teacher was having problems with a particular student and was willing to try anything. Liz spotted the student immediately. She was a tall, over-aged student, and she had a way of making her presence known, to put it mildly. She was out of her seat, walking around, blurting out answers, picking on other students, etc. Following the observation, Liz asked the teacher for permission to speak to this particular student. Liz called the student out of the room, and the student followed, surmising that she was "in trouble." Liz introduced herself and said to the student, "I'm Mrs. Yates, and I work for the school board. I couldn't help noticing some things about your behavior." Now the student *really* assumed that she was in trouble! Liz went on to say, "I noticed that you have a way of standing out in a crowd. You've got some real leadership potential!" The student, dumbfounded, listened attentively. "I also noticed," said Liz, "that you're very knowledgeable." (You see, she had noted that even though the student was "blurting out" answers, the answers were correct!) "Have you ever thought about being a teacher when you grow up?" asked Liz. "You know, if you could learn to temper your behavior a little, I think that both you and others would really benefit from your skills and abilities. You've got some real possibilities." The student thanked Liz profusely and went back into the classroom. Liz told the teacher about how she had handled the situation, and the teacher decided to give that same "psychology" a try. Six months later, Liz went back into the same classroom. When Liz entered, the student ran up to her, called her by name, hugged her, and said, "I've decided to be a teacher, and I've really been practicing hard!" The teacher told Liz that the child had become a model student. "She participates in class, she behaves very well, she's working on managing her tendency to express her opinions inappropriately, and she now stays in at recess to tutor the same students she used to tease. I can't believe the difference, and I'm amazed at what a little psychology can accomplish!" said the teacher.

Using clever psychology can be both fascinating and fun! Of course, the right psychology requires the right attitude. Any effective teacher will tell you that "attitude" will make or break you in the classroom. So adopt the attitude of helping students to help themselves. Be resolved to turn potentially negative situations into positive ones. Model an attitude of optimism. Convince students that you believe in them—especially when they are having trouble believing in themselves. Go ahead and give it a try. You have nothing to lose, and your students have everything to gain.

"Act enthusiastic and you become enthusiastic."

Dale Carnegie

Act as though Every Subject You Teach Is Your "Favorite"

How often have we heard a teacher say to students, "Well, word problems were never my favorite either, but we have to do them, so let's get busy with them." Once I heard a teacher announce to her class, "Look, I'm not very good at writing essays either, so we'll be learning together." Imagine a doctor saying to you, the patient, "Look, your particular illness is my least favorite to treat, but you're sick, so let's see what we can do…" or better yet, "I'm not a very good surgeon so we'll be learning together!" Now please do not misunderstand. I am in no way suggesting that "acting" enthusiastic is enough. No "enthusiastic" surgeon will operate on me unless he is highly qualified! However, I do want to feel that my highly qualified surgeon enjoys what he does and thereby continues to improve his skills. By the same token, "acting" enthusiastic in the classroom is not enough. You must be, of course, highly qualified to teach the subject matter. However, being highly qualified without being highly enthusiastic will not make for successful teaching. It is true that every subject we teach may not be our favorite. The trick is not to announce that to your students. You see, student enthusiasm tends to mirror teacher enthusiasm. If you should ever doubt this, follow a group of students from an enthusiastic teacher's classroom to a nonenthusiastic teacher's classroom. You'll witness an entirely different group of students, or so it will seem. So be the most enthusiastic person you know with whatever you teach.

> **"Keep your face to the sunshine and you cannot see the shadows."**

> Helen Keller

Focus on the "Positives" in Your Classroom

I once watched a motivational speaker make a profound statement to his audience with the use of an activity. He had the audience look around the room. They had thirty seconds to locate and commit to memory as many things as they saw that were yellow—any shade of yellow. The activity began, and the eyes of the participants quickly scanned the room for yellow objects. At the end of the thirty seconds, he had them close their eyes. He then said, "Okay, make a mental list of everything in this room that is black. The participants, stunned, could not remember one thing that was black. (Their eyes were still closed.) He then had them open their eyes and look around once more. Everyone was amazed at the fact that there were many more black objects than there were yellow. However, because they had focused on the yellow, that's all they had seen. Point? "Keep your face to the sunshine (yellow) and you cannot see the shadows (black)." The speaker related this activity to life—that life is what we focus on. I will relate that same principle to the classroom. In our classrooms, at any given time, there are probably as many negatives (black) as there are positives (yellow). If we look hard enough, we will find something negative, if that's where we place our focus. The good news is that the same holds true for the positives in our classrooms. It's all too easy, at times, to get frustrated and begin focusing in on "all that's wrong." These are phrases you will hear often in the classroom of someone focusing on negatives: "Don't do that." "Sit down." "Sit up straight." "Stop it." "Uh, would you mind paying attention?" "You are not supposed to be talking." "Get quiet." "If you do it one more time…" "Don't make me have to send you to the principal." Interestingly, students do tend to live up to the expectations of their teachers, so inappropriate behaviors are actually being encouraged in this type of classroom. Conversely, these are phrases you will hear often in the classroom of someone focusing on positives: "Thank you for raising your hand." "Great job!" "I appreciate your attentiveness to this important task." "I'm so proud of you." Once again, students tend to meet our expectations, so in this case, positive behaviors are being encouraged. This is not to suggest, of course, that nothing negative ever happens in the classroom of a positive teacher. However, these incidences are rare and are dealt with in a respectful manner, therefore encouraging, once again, positive behaviors.

Effective teachers know that focusing on the positives (yellow) in their classrooms will foster positive behaviors, overshadowing and eventually obliterating the darkness.

FACT: Students like to see their work displayed. In a classroom where student work is "everywhere," students feel a sense of both pride and ownership.

Display Student Work

During a recent visit to a ninth-grade science class, I immediately noticed that the classroom walls consisted of nothing but student work and pictures of students working. The teacher said to the students, "Tell Ms. Breaux about what we've been learning." They immediately began pointing to their projects around the room and their work samples on the walls. After remarking about one particular project, a student quickly led me to the pictures taken while the students were completing the project—a chronological photographic display of every step of the process. The students went on and on and wanted to show me everything and tell me about all they had been doing. The teacher made no attempt to stop them, for which I was glad. He simply let them display their accomplishments with pride. One of the students even suggested getting a photograph of them explaining their work to me. The teacher readily picked up his camera and snapped a few shots while the students continued to speak of their accomplishments. Then one student said, "Oh, let me show a picture of the experiment that didn't work." He quickly led me to a photograph, and beneath it was a poster entitled, "What We Learned From This Mistake."

The teacher shared with me afterward that the classroom belonged to everyone, so he believed in giving everyone equal ownership. "Notice," he said, "that everyone has work displayed. That's because every student experiences success in my room. But also notice that there are no graded assignments up on the walls. If I did that, only the brightest students would ever have their work displayed. I want everyone's work up there, and they all want their work up there, too. For some, it's the first time they've ever had any of their work displayed for all to see and enjoy. I've also noticed that the more pictures I take, the harder they work. They love to see pictures of themselves working."

When asked what advice he would give to other teachers about displaying student work, he smiled and said, "Display lots of student work in the classroom, and turn every learning opportunity into a 'Kodak' moment."

> **"Treat people as if they were what they ought to be and you help them to become what they are capable of becoming."**
>
> Johann Wolfgang von Goethe

Have Positive Expectations for *All* Students

Many years back, I had an experience with a student that I will never forget. It was the week before school began, and I attended a meeting for parents and teachers. The parents of Raneesha said to me, "We're apologizing in advance for Raneesha's attitude." "What do you mean?" I asked. I had not even met Raneesha yet. "Well, she's got a real attitude problem. Any teacher who's ever taught her can tell you that, and we see it at home every day. We tell her that her attitude is bad, but that doesn't change her. Just let us know when she gets out of line, and we'll deal with her." Knowing that I needed to address that situation from day one, I decided that I would find any opportunity to "capitalize" on any hint of a positive attitude I could manage to find in Raneesha. I was a little apprehensive about meeting her, to be quite honest. Yet, I was determined to have high expectations. On the first day of school, Raneesha walked into my classroom. I introduced myself, and she reluctantly shook my hand. I then said, "You look like someone I can trust. Would you please bring this very important envelope to the secretary for me?" (The envelope was empty, and the secretary already knew to expect it.) "Yes ma'am," answered Raneesha, with a hint of a smile on her face. "Thank you so much," I responded. "I like your smile, I like your manners, and I love your attitude!" I said. From that moment on, Raneesha displayed a "model" attitude in my classroom. But I never let up on mentioning her positive attitude to her as often as possible. About six weeks later, Raneesha stayed after class one day to hand me a letter from her parents. "What's this?" I asked. "It's a letter from my parents. They wanted to tell you that my attitude has improved a lot at home, and they want to thank you for helping me with that." Acting totally oblivious to her past history, I said, "What do you mean by improved? How could your attitude possibly improve? You've got one of the best attitudes I've ever seen in a seventh grader." Raneesha went on to explain to me what I already knew—the fact that her attitude had previously left a lot to be desired, both at home and at school. "So, why the sudden change?" I asked. "Well, I thought about that a lot," said Raneesha. "Remember on the first day of school when you told me I had a good attitude? I guess I figured you didn't know any better and that maybe I did have a good attitude hidden inside of me somewhere. You were the first person that ever told me anything positive about my attitude. It was like you just expected me to have a good attitude, so I did."

This is just one small, yet profound, example of how students will live up to your expectations. If you treat students as if you expect them to be successful, whether it is in their studies or in their dealings with others, and if you start with very small successes and capitalize on those as opposed to reinforcing negative expectations, then they will truly become what they are capable of becoming! Just as we tend to get out of life what we expect out of life, we tend to get out of our students what we expect out of our students.

> *If I knew you and you knew me,*
> *If both of us could clearly see,*
> *And with an inner sight divine,*
> *The meaning of your heart and mine,*
> *I'm sure that we would differ less*
> *And clasp our hands in friendliness,*
> *Our thoughts would pleasantly agree*
> *If I knew you and you knew me.*
>
> Nixon Waterman

Get to Know Your Students

A coworker of mine was recently called in to observe a classroom teacher who was having a few management problems. The biggest "problem" of all was with a student named Ricardo, who simply did not do much of his work. As my coworker entered the room, the teacher pointed out Ricardo. He was seated in the back of the room, so my coworker took a seat not far from him. She immediately noticed that he had a large cast on his arm from his shoulder to his hand. There were even metal pins sticking out at the elbow. He had obviously had some type of terrible accident. After class, my coworker asked the teacher, "What happened to Ricardo's arm?" "I don't know," said the teacher. "Didn't you ask him?" inquired my coworker. "I teach 92 students a day," said the teacher. "I don't have time to know anything personal about any of them. All I have time to do is teach!" And this, of course, is why the teacher was having management problems. My coworker recalled that at no time was there any real interaction between the teacher and any of her students. She lectured, and they took notes. Believe it or not, Ricardo was even trying to take notes with his left hand, but he soon gave up. Ricardo needed some help. He deserved to have his notes "given" to him. He deserved to have a teacher who took an interest in what had happened to him. He deserved to have a teacher who cared about him as a person. So did all of the other students.

It is of utmost importance that teachers get to know something about each of their students. Remember that students, of any age, who believe that you genuinely care about them as people will give you their best efforts in order to please you. No, you cannot know everything there is to know about every student, but knowing "something" about each of them is easily attainable and highly beneficial.

Good news: This teacher took the advice of my coworker. She got to know her students more personally and began interacting with them more in her teaching. Her management problems have decreased drastically. Ricardo's arm has healed beautifully, and he now uses it to do his work in class.

Babe Ruth, in his career, hit 714 homeruns. He also struck out 1330 times!

Encourage Improvement, Not Perfection

In the sport of baseball, many, many of the "greats" have made it into the Hall of Fame with a .300 lifetime batting average or less. That means that they "failed" 70 percent of the time! Yet they are considered extremely successful—the best of the best. In school, however, you have to succeed at least 70 percent of the time in order to barely get by with a passing grade. Try to imagine *any* area of your life where you are successful more than 70 percent of the time. I'll bet you'll have a difficult time doing that. In football, every single play is technically designed to score points. However, almost every play does *not* score points. That doesn't stop the coach from working from each play that does not score points and trying to turn the next play into a more successful one, however. Find a parent who succeeds 70 percent of the time with everything he tries to teach his child. That parent does not exist. Better yet, find a stockbroker who succeeds with 70 percent of all of his stock trades! If you do, call me. I'll invest!

The point is that we often label students as failures because we are making the mistake of encouraging perfection in all of them. This is the way we were "trained" to think in school. Admit it—if you took a test with 100 questions and received a grade of 95 percent, you would immediately look for the five that you missed as opposed to the 95 that you got right! And many of you would be upset with anything less than 100 percent. In a conversation with a teacher, I learned that she had many students who were experiencing what she called "no success at all." In looking more closely at the situation, I learned that these students were struggling with content that was way above their levels. And amazingly, they were managing to score 50 percent or better on her tests. I saw some real potential here, and I shared my observations with this teacher. I said, "I'm going to speak to you in Chinese and I'm going to teach you in Chinese and then I'll test you in Chinese. What do you think you'll score?" "Well, I don't know how to speak Chinese, so I'll score a zero," she said. (Neither do I speak Chinese, by the way, but I was just trying to make a point.) "Don't you think you could at least get half of all the answers correct?" I asked. "No way," she said. "Well, what you're trying to teach these particular struggling students is material that's far above their levels of understanding. It's almost as if you were speaking and teaching and testing in a language that is foreign to them. Yet they're getting at least half of it correct. Wow! What potential!" I exclaimed. "I never thought of it that way," said the teacher. "I think I see where you're going with this. I need to speak in 'their' language, at 'their' levels." "Absolutely," I answered. "And then move them forward from there. You'll be amazed at their progress, based on their potential and their obvious tendencies to be overachievers!" I added.

The teacher began, the very next day, to teach these students from their current levels of understanding. Then, she agreed that she would focus only on improvement, not perfection. Within a few weeks, these students had made enormous strides. By the end of the semester, every single one of them was able to pass the course. No, they did not make straight A's, but they did pass. And they were experiencing success unlike any they had ever experienced.

In the classroom, we should teach students that improvement is what matters. Perfection is not only impossible, but striving for it will give you ulcers and will drive the people around you out of their minds! Success is attainable for anyone, one step at a time. Homeruns are great, but strikeouts are opportunities to improve your skills. An enthusiastic "swing and a miss" has led many people to greatness.

> **"The inner landscape of many children is full of mines ready to explode upon careless contact. Any insulting remark can set off an explosion."**
>
> Haim Ginott

Avoid Sarcasm

"What time is it?" asked a student. "I'll tell you what time it is. It's time for you to be quiet," answered the teacher, in a less than pleasant tone. Having been seated in the classroom for about 15 minutes, I knew that this student had been busily and quietly at work. "Why the sarcasm?" I wondered. A few minutes later, most of the students had finished their assignments. Naturally, some of them began whispering to one another. "Excuse me!" barked the teacher. You're supposed to be working, not talking." "We're finished," said some of the students. "Well, I had better not find any mistakes on your papers," answered the teacher. "I can't figure out problem 4," said another student. "Well, maybe if the rest of your classmates would be engaging their brains instead of their mouths, you might be able to concentrate better," huffed the teacher. By this point, almost everyone was talking. The teacher got angrier and became more sarcastic, which finally led to a hostile confrontation with a student. "Open your mouth one more time, and you're going straight to the office," yelled the teacher. "I'm not going to the office unless everyone else goes," said the student, "because they're all talking, too!"

This situation, of course, went from bad to worse. And this teacher felt victimized by her students. In actuality, however, her negative tone and sarcastic words were provoking the same behaviors in her students—not to mention the fact that there was too much "down" time where students had nothing to do. Therefore, her lack of management led to talking which made her angry and evoked sarcasm. But regardless of what came first, the fact is that this teacher was using sarcasm, and there is simply no place for sarcasm in the classroom. Sarcasm accomplishes nothing positive, it's completely unprofessional, and it shows a lack of control on the part of the teacher. Most students in our classrooms have to deal with enough cynicism already in their lives. We, as teachers, are supposed to lift them, to build their self-esteem, to encourage their endeavors, and to model appropriate behavior. Using sarcasm will help to accomplish none of these things.

What time is it? It's time for all of us to take a good look at our behaviors with students and refrain from using any kind of comments that may even "hint" of sarcasm.

FACT: Most students think you are something other than human. If they see you out in public, they're amazed that you don't "live" in your classroom!

Be "Human" to Your Students

If you have ever encountered one of your students in the grocery store or at a social function, then you know that the above "fact" is true. It's almost as though you're a celebrity when you're recognized by your students outside of school. "Wow! She actually shops for groceries!" Students don't automatically see you as "human." They see you as their teacher, period. And though there is a fine line that you do not want to cross, you do want to become as human as possible to your students.

In the book, *The First Days of School*,* teachers are encouraged to create a personality bulletin board. We implement this suggestion in many of our schools, and the students love it. All it requires is making a bulletin board about yourself. Items on the bulletin board may include: your hobbies, your interests, pictures of you when you were in school, your school report cards, your family's pictures, awards you have received, your diplomas, etc. It's such a simple idea, and it truly makes a big difference in becoming "human" to your students. Give it a try. Be human to your students, and they will respect you more. Students need to know that you, too, are a living, breathing individual who possibly made less-than-perfect grades when you were in school!

* Wong, H. K., & Wong, R. T. (1998). *The first days of school: How to be an effective teacher.* Mountain View, CA: Harry K. Wong Publications.

Tip 86

Definitions:
1st person—person speaking (I, me, my, mine, etc.)
2nd person—person spoken to (you, your, yours, etc.)
3rd person—person spoken of (she, he, it, they, etc.)

Refer to Yourself in the "First Person"

To emphasize the point I'm trying to make, I'm going to speak to you, here, in the third person. Now imagine that you are in the room with me, and I begin speaking to you in this way: Ms. Breaux is very glad that you're reading Ms. Breaux's book. She hopes that it will benefit you in improving your teaching. She really wants for you to pay special attention to what is meant by speaking in the first person.

Wouldn't it seem strange that I'm referring to myself almost as if I'm not there or as if I'm speaking of someone else? What comes naturally is to say, "I'm very glad that you're reading my book. I hope that it will benefit you in improving your teaching. I really want for you to pay special attention to what is meant by speaking in the first person."

Okay, so why is it that teachers tend to speak to their students using the third person when speaking of themselves? It sounds like this: "Good morning, students. Ms. Breaux wants for you to take out your language books. Ms. Breaux will be showing you how to _____." I know you'll recognize it, because it's definitely a "teacher" thing. I have yet to hear anyone in any other profession refer to himself or herself in the third person. What teachers don't realize is that it sounds condescending and it creates a "distance" or "barrier" between them and their students when they say things like, "Ms. Breaux is very proud of you," or "Ms. Breaux doesn't like the way you're behaving." I have found that many teachers do this unconsciously. It's a "learned" habit. So give it some thought, and recognize whether or not you tend to speak this way in your classroom. If you do, you may want to rethink it. Speaking in the first person is modeling "natural" speech, and it also makes your conversations with others more personal.

Ms. Breaux is now finished discussing Ms. Breaux's point here.

> "Life is a great bundle of little things."
>
> Oliver Wendell Holmes, Sr.

Remember that Little Things Make a Big Difference

We often hear it said and know it to be true that the little things in life make the biggest difference. A simple pat on the back or a smile might be just what someone needs to brighten his day. In the classroom, little things make a big difference to your students. And by the way, they cost nothing. A Family and Consumer Sciences teacher shared the following story: "We were baking a cake as a class, and since it happened to be Mary's birthday, I dedicated the cake to her. After class, this 13-year-old thanked me and told me that it was the first birthday cake she had ever received! And I realized what a big difference that one small gesture had made."

Here is a list of a few little things that will make a big difference to your students:

- ◆ Acknowledge student birthdays.
- ◆ Greet each student as they enter your classroom with a smile.
- ◆ Compliment students on jobs well done.
- ◆ Make a positive phone call to a parent to tell him about something his child has accomplished in your classroom.
- ◆ Write encouraging comments on student work.
- ◆ Visit a sick student in the hospital, or at least make a phone call.
- ◆ Write a thank-you note to a student who has given you a gift.
- ◆ Notice new haircuts.
- ◆ Attend school functions to show support.
- ◆ Ask students about their hobbies and interests.
- ◆ Notice and encourage even the smallest of student successes.

Though this list is by no means all-inclusive, it reminds us of the little things that we often tend to overlook. Remember to do the little things, and you will reap the benefits of making big differences in the lives of your students.

FACT: If you maintain a child's dignity, you will see lasting results. If you take away a child's dignity, you may face lasting revenge.

Dignify Incorrect Responses

In Teaching Tip 18, we discuss the importance of avoiding power struggles with students. It has been my observation that teachers often engage in power struggles with students when students either do not know the answer to a question or, better yet, when they give a "ridiculous" answer intentionally. Here's an actual classroom example. The class was discussing United States presidents. The teacher asked, "Who was our first president?" One student in the back of the room raised his hand and answered, "David Letterman." The students, of course, found this quite amusing. The teacher now had a choice. She could enter into a power struggle and show frustration and aggravation, or she could take all energy away from the student, discreetly discouraging that type of answer, maintaining her composure, and still managing to maintain the student's dignity. Had she chosen to "play," she would have probably said the following, in a tone of frustration and aggravation: "Very funny. Are you finished with your comedy routine? You know darned good and well that the first president was not David Letterman! Now if you can't give serious answers, don't give any at all." This, of course, would have added more fuel to the fire, increasing the likelihood of the same behavior in the future. However, this teacher amazed me as she looked at the student reassuringly and said, "I know exactly what you're thinking. You're thinking of a male, and both David Letterman and the first president are males, and you're thinking of a famous person, and both of these men are famous. Good thinking. Now can someone tell me the name of the first president?" What happened was that another student answered correctly, and the student with the "sarcastic" answer was completely defused. He looked a little shocked, thinking that his answer was not so far off after all, as his teacher had just given him some credit. For the remainder of the discussion, he remained actively involved, and on two occasions, he volunteered more "serious" answers.

Following the lesson, I commended the teacher on the way she had handled that situation. She said, "Oh. Well, he's a new student, and he's just trying to fit in. So I'm going to do my best to see that he does fit in, but in a positive way. Besides that, I never give any energy to those kinds of things. I've got bigger fish to fry!"

On the very same day, I was observing in another classroom where one of the students gave an incorrect answer, but not an intentionally incorrect an-

Tip 89

swer. This teacher responded by saying, "We've been talking about this for a week now. Where have you been?" I was appalled, but more important was the fact that this poor student was embarrassed. What this student did for the rest of the class period was absolutely nothing. She shut down completely and was reprimanded once again by the teacher. This time, it was for being inattentive.

When students shut down, we lose them. And if we are the cause of that "shutting down," then we are facing inevitable discipline problems atop the inevitable academic problems. Students may give incorrect answers, but at least they're participating! And those incorrect answers assist us in monitoring their understanding or lack of understanding of a concept. The secret is to dignify incorrect responses, whether intentional or not. When students feel that they are treated with respect and dignity, teachers see lasting, positive results. When the opposite is the case, teachers are setting themselves up to face lasting revenge.

> *Teach me to feel another's woe,*
> *To hide the faults I see;*
> *That mercy I to others show,*
> *That mercy show to me.*
>
> Alexander Pope

Avoid "Nagging"

The best way to describe "nagging" is by defining it, in teacher terms. Nagging means taking way too long to make a point that could have been stated in a few words. Here's an example: A student has had difficulty turning in homework assignments. One day, she brings in an assignment on time. A "nagging" teacher says, "Mary, why can't you bring in your assignments on time every day? If you can do it once, you can do it again. Doesn't it feel good to have your assignment turned in on time? If you would only do this every time, I wouldn't have to punish you and constantly be on your back about it. Then we'd both be happier. I'm hoping you've learned a lesson from this. Have you?" Do you notice how the teacher goes on and on and on? That's nagging. Now let's look at the same situation from a non-nagging standpoint. "Great, Mary. Thanks for bringing your assignment in on time. I'm so proud of you." This scenario is an example of encouraging the student as opposed to nagging the student. Students respond much better to encouragement than they do to nagging. (So do adults!) Now, in order not to sound like I'm nagging you about nagging, I'll end this section because I've made my point!

Tip 90

> "Laughter is the shortest distance between two people."

Victor Borge

Laugh with Your Students

Many studies have been conducted on laughter and many books have been written on the subject. Basically, they all say the same thing: Laughter is the best medicine! It has been proven that laughing releases endorphins in the brain that boost our immune systems and make us happier people in general. Laughing feels good. Environments where laughter abounds are happy places. I once read a study that showed that on the average, children laugh several hundred times a day as opposed to adults who laugh less than twenty! Maybe that's why children are happier and healthier than adults! Students love teachers who laugh with them. Yes, there are times when laughter is not appropriate. That's common sense. But when the opportunity presents itself—and it will present itself often in the classroom—have a good laugh with your students.

Regrettably, many teachers will readily admit that they don't laugh very often in the classroom. I once asked a teacher why she felt this was so, and she answered, "Because teaching is serious business!" Needless to say, she was struggling desperately with managing student behavior. The students were not having fun with the teacher, so they decided to have fun without her! You were supposed to laugh at that. Did you?

Is your glass half empty or half full?

Be an Optimist

Consider the following two poems, and decide whether your glass is half empty or half full...

> ### Oh, Woe Is Me
>
> *Oh, woe is me, I am a teacher*
> *Parent, doctor, therapist, preacher*
> *Battling daily with the youth*
> *Whose attitudes are more than uncouth*
> *A disciplinarian, no stranger to force*
> *Don't talk to me after 3:30—I'm hoarse*
> *One year of experience 20 times o'er*
> *I teach each year like the year before*
> *My students are disrespectful and lazy*
> *Yet they look at me like I am crazy*
> *If it weren't for students, my life would be swell*
> *And my job wouldn't seem like a living hell*
> *Speaking of which, I've gotta go*
> *My principal's coming—gotta put on a show!*
>
> Annette L. Breaux

I Teach

I light a spark in a darkened soul
I warm the heart of one grown cold
I look beyond and see within
Behind the face, beneath the skin
I quench a thirst, I soothe a pain
I provide the food that will sustain
I touch, I love, I laugh, I cry
Whatever is needed, I supply
Yet more than I give, I gain from each
I am most richly blessed—I teach!

Annette L. Breaux

Be an OPTIMIST!!!

> "The deepest principle of human nature is the craving to be appreciated."

William James

Thank Your Students Often

In Tip 88, we discuss the fact that little things make a big difference to students. Saying "thank you" is one of the little things we can do that will make a big difference. Here are some of the benefits of saying thank you:

- It's free.
- It tells students that you care.
- It makes students feel appreciated and special.
- It models appropriate manners.
- It encourages students to do better, to be better.
- It sets a tone of encouragement in the classroom.
- It promotes an overall positive learning environment.

I had the privilege of observing a teacher who thanks her students often—more often, in fact, than any teacher I've ever observed. Here are some of the things I heard during this observation: "Thank you for getting to work so quickly." "Thank you for sharing that with us." "Thank you for understanding that we cannot chew gum in class." (This was said to a student who *was* chewing gum. She immediately disposed of the gum.) "Thank you for not bringing the problems from recess into the classroom. I know it's a really difficult thing to do. If you want to discuss it, we'll do that after class. Thanks for understanding that." (This was said to a student who *was* bringing his problems from recess into the classroom. He immediately got quiet.) "Thank you for that answer." "Thank you for making that mistake. We can all learn from it." "Thank you for remembering to bring in your homework." "Thanks for your help."

I later learned, not to my surprise, that this teacher had almost zero discipline problems. Is it any wonder? And yet, she had lots of "tough" students in her classes every year. In her classroom, however, her students were successful, they were polite, they worked diligently, and they absolutely loved her.

Remember, saying thank you doesn't cost a thing, yet the rewards are truly priceless. Thank your students often!

Tip 93

A Teacher's Influence

> "A teacher affects eternity. He can never tell where his influence stops."

> Henry B. Adams

Recognize the Importance of Your Influence

Most teachers choose the teaching profession as the result of the influence of one or two teachers who inspired them somewhere along the way. And, plentiful are the stories of children's lives being positively impacted and sometimes literally saved because of the influence of a teacher. I know that I would not have chosen the teaching profession, nor would I be writing this book, were it not for the influence of my fourth-grade teacher, Sr. Naoma Duhe, my fifth-grade teacher, Sr. Martha Richard, and my ninth-grade English teacher, Mrs. Marge Barker, who influenced not only the person I was then, but the person I am now, and the person that I will become. You see, whether we deserve it or not, our students think that we "hang the moon," unless we give them reason to believe otherwise. So make a sincere effort to realize that your influence is one of great importance in the eyes of your students. If you impact the life of one student in a positive way, you therefore influence the person that he becomes, which will affect the life of every person he ever encounters. You will never fully realize the magnitude of your influence. But know, today and every day, that all of your actions and reactions with your students will help to determine the type of influence you will have on them—not just for today, but for the rest of their lives.

Tip 94

> **"A child's life is like a piece of paper on which every passerby leaves a mark."**
>
> Chinese Proverb

Realize that You Will Affect Lives

As teachers, as everyday, normal, run-of-the-mill individuals, we often tend to underestimate the fact that we truly do affect the lives of every student we teach. This influence can be very powerful—hopefully in a positive sense—yet it can also be very harmful if we do not treat this "power" with the utmost reverence and respect. You see, it is often easy to say things out of frustration—things that we may think nothing of, but that students will internalize and take to heart. A teacher recently shared an experience with me. She said, "I'm an accomplished musician. I teach at the university level, I perform, and I have been quite successful in my career. Isn't it sad that I cannot even balance a checkbook? And it's all because of my fifth-grade teacher." "What do you mean?" I asked. "Well," she said, "I remember it like it was yesterday. I was standing at the board, struggling to work through a math problem. The teacher was so frustrated with me, and she let the whole class know it. She told me I would never be any good at math. Guess what? I never was. It affected me so intensely that I developed a mental block when it came to math, and I've struggled with it all my life." Ironically, she recently received a letter from one of her former music students who said, "How often we underestimate the power of words. I will never forget the five words you spoke to me which have stayed with me all my life. The words were, 'I'm so proud of you.'" So from one individual's story comes a perfect example of both the positive and the negative power of a teacher's influence.

The fact is that you, as a teacher, will influence the life of every single student you teach. Whether that influence is positive or negative is completely up to you!

> "The mediocre teacher tells. The good teacher explains. The superior teacher demonstrates. The great teacher inspires."

William Arthur Ward

Remember Your "Favorite" Teacher

Call up a mental image of your all-time, absolute favorite teacher. We all had one. Got it? If you do, you're probably already smiling at this point. Okay, before you read any further, make a list of several characteristics of that teacher, including what made him or her your favorite. Do not read on until you do this. Remember, if you told your students not to read on and they did anyway, you would be upset. So, practice what you preach, stop reading, and make that list.

I have conducted this activity with thousands of teachers over the years and will share some commonalities in their lists. I'll bet that you'll see more than a few similarities with your own list.

- My favorite teacher was a nice person.
- My favorite teacher made me feel special.
- My favorite teacher smiled a lot.
- My favorite teacher had a way of making me succeed.
- My favorite teacher made learning fun.
- My favorite teacher did not yell at me or embarrass me in front of others.
- My favorite teacher treated students respectfully.
- My favorite teacher did not struggle with discipline problems.
- My favorite teacher inspired me in so many ways.
- My favorite teacher could make anything seem interesting.
- My favorite teacher really loved teaching.
- My favorite teacher really loved children.

Did you find some of the same things you listed? Notice that nothing in that list mentions the teacher's credentials. I have yet to find someone to say, "My favorite teacher had three college degrees." And notice that nothing in that list tells of the amount of material that the teacher had students memorize. And take special notice that the list tends to focus on the teacher as a "person" and how that teacher made students "feel" as people—special, loved, successful, and inspired.

Question: Would your students write similar things about you?

Remember: By the very nature of your position, you will influence the lives of every student you teach. Whether that influence is a positive or a negative one, it will most certainly be a lasting one!

Remember Your "Least-Favorite" Teacher

In the previous tip, I had you list the characteristics of your favorite teacher. This time, we will repeat the same process, except that you will be listing the characteristics of your least-favorite teacher. Remember not to read on until you have called up the image of this person and listed several characteristics. Okay, get busy making your list.

Just as in the previous tip, I have conducted this activity with thousands of teachers over the years, and there are uncanny similarities in their lists. Once again, I'll bet that you'll see more than a few similarities with your own list.

- ◆ My least-favorite teacher was not a very nice person.
- ◆ My least-favorite teacher did not make me feel special.
- ◆ My least-favorite teacher rarely smiled.
- ◆ My least-favorite teacher didn't care if I succeeded or not.
- ◆ My least-favorite teacher's class was boring.
- ◆ My least-favorite teacher yelled at students and embarrassed them.
- ◆ My least-favorite teacher treated students disrespectfully.
- ◆ My least-favorite teacher had lots of discipline problems.
- ◆ My least-favorite teacher did not inspire me.
- ◆ My least-favorite teacher didn't make the subject matter interesting.
- ◆ My least-favorite teacher seemed to dislike teaching.
- ◆ My least-favorite teacher seemed to dislike children.

Note that the above are in direct opposition to the "favorite" teacher characteristics in the previous tip. Also note that your feelings about your least-favorite teacher are the antithesis of your feelings about your favorite teacher. I have often seen adults conjure up real anger during this exercise when they think of their least-favorite teacher. Most can remember, in the minutest of detail, some specific things that this teacher said or did to hurt or upset them. Usually, these are things that happened many years ago, yet just thinking about their least-favorite teacher brings them right back to those unpleasant feelings, as if the situations were happening all over again. Also, I have yet to find anyone participating in this exercise who says the following: "My least-favorite teacher really inspired me, but I just didn't like him." The fact is that if you can succeed in convincing a student that you care, and if you can inspire him, you will always fall into the favorite-teacher category. Not that we're competing in any kind of "popularity" contest here, because we aren't. What we're doing is much more significant than being popular. We're affecting lives and leaving our indelible marks on every student who enters our classroom doors. None of us wants to be remembered in the "least-favorite" category. So keep in mind your least-favorite teacher, keep in mind your favorite teacher, and use their lessons to make it abundantly clear what you do and do *not* want to represent in your students' lives. Remember, your influence will long outlive you. Leave a positive legacy.

> *If you plan for a year, plant a seed.*
> *If for ten years, plant a tree.*
> *If for a hundred years, teach the people.*
> *When you sow a seed once, you will reap a single harvest.*
> *When you teach the people, you will reap a hundred harvests.*
>
> Kuan Chung

Inspire for a Lifetime

Students are much more in need of inspiration than of information. The information we provide is important, but the inspiration we provide is life altering. An inspired individual will achieve great things. An informed individual will accomplish nothing if he lacks inspiration.

In the conclusion, you will read a beautiful example of how one teacher literally changed the entire life of a student without knowing it until years later. We will never know how many lives have been influenced through our teaching, but we can rest assured that our influence as teachers is lifelong, and it is important that we recognize and capitalize on that fact. If you inspire one student, you affect his entire future, and you literally change the world. You, as a teacher, have the opportunity, through your actions, to inspire every student who ever walks through your classroom doors, thereby changing this world, one student at a time. What an awesome responsibility! May you never take it lightly.

> "In my heart, I know that teaching is more than just a career. It's a vocation. Oftentimes, I stop and wonder if I'm really making a difference. Then I take out my 'I Am Special' folder and look through the things the students have given to me over the years. It's amazing that no matter how many difficulties we may encounter, one student's success or gratitude can wash all the negatives away. So every year, I give 'I Am Special' folders to the new teachers, and I put their first note of gratitude in it, thanking them for choosing to make a difference. They have no idea how that folder will fill up in no time!"
>
> Noelee Brooks, Principal

Keep an "I Am Special" Folder

Whether you are a new teacher or a seasoned veteran, it's never too late to start keeping an "I Am Special" folder. It's a very simple concept with very special rewards. An "I Am Special" folder is a folder where you will keep notes from students, thank-you cards, letters of appreciation, notes to yourself on something exciting or heartwarming that happens to you on a particular day, letters from parents, etc. And on those really difficult days when you are questioning whether you truly are making a difference, just take out the folder and begin to look through it. It will reaffirm the fact that you are making a difference, it will rekindle your love of children and of teaching, and it will remind you that you have truly chosen the most noble of all professions—teaching!

As teachers, we are special to so many students. But sometimes we need a reminder. An "I Am Special" folder will do the trick!

> "The greatest mistake a person can make is to be afraid of making one."

> Elbert Hubbard

Teach Students that Mistakes Are Wonderful Learning Opportunities

What happened to you the first time you tried to ride a bicycle on your own? You fell. What happened the first time you tried to tie your own shoelaces? It didn't "quite" work out. And here's one we can all relate to: What is typically the first word that a baby speaks? "Da-da." Okay, I've checked the dictionary, and there's no such word. In other words, the baby makes a "mistake." And what do we do, as parents? We praise the mistake and tell the baby to say it again. We call everyone we know to tell them that our baby has spoken his first word. We encourage the mistake. We videotape the mistake. We even go so far as to start making the mistake ourselves, saying, "Where's da-da?" "Say da-da." We would never dream of saying "No, don't say that," to the baby. And we definitely would not ever think of labeling him a "nontalker." This is because parents know that this "mistake" is a necessary part of the process of learning to speak. All parents know that the "mistake" will eventually correct itself, so not only do they not worry about it, but they actually encourage the child's many mistakes as he learns to speak. Oh, and the good news is that I have yet to meet an adult who still calls his father "da-da."

Isn't it true that we learn best through our mistakes? Skinned knees are a necessary part to learning to ride a bike. Burnt meals are a necessary part of learning to cook. Now think back to your first year of teaching. Did you make mistakes? In fact, no matter how long you've been teaching, don't you still make mistakes? So why is it that in many classrooms, mistakes are quickly marked with a red "X"? Why is it that we don't hear enough teachers saying, "Great! You made a mistake. Now let's see what we can learn from it." Even though we know, as adults, that mistakes are wonderful learning opportunities, this is not the prevailing message in many classrooms. Understand that I am not suggesting that we never point out a student's mistakes. I am, rather, suggesting that we make it "okay" to make a mistake in our classrooms. Because making mistakes is one of the ways that we learn best, we should actually encourage students to go ahead, take risks, make mistakes, and then learn from them. No student should ever be singled out and embarrassed for making a mistake. The greatest mistake any student can make is to stop trying for fear of failing. And the greatest mistake any teacher can make is to encourage that type of behavior. Any environment conducive to learning is one where students feel comfortable enough to simply do their best—no matter the outcome.

> **"The good teacher makes the poor student good and the good student superior. When our students fail, we, as teachers, have failed."**
>
> Marva Collins

Refuse to Give Up on Any Child

It is when we think we have exhausted all resources that we should resolve never to stop trying. It is when a child tries our patience to the very end that we must muster even more patience. It is when we think we can't that we should. It should be with utmost resolve that we refuse to give up on any student. It should be with resolute determination that we commit to making every child successful, no matter what it takes. And when a child is not experiencing success, we, as teachers, must change our approach—and keep changing that approach until we find one that works.

Remember the following:

- Every child is someone special.
- Every child deserves a fair chance.
- Every child deserves a capable, caring, competent teacher.
- Every child deserves to be treated with dignity and respect.
- Every child is capable of success.
- Every child has strengths that need to be recognized and nurtured.
- Every child truly wants to succeed.
- Every child craves love and appreciation—which every teacher should provide.

Find the beauty in each child that often lies hidden behind life's layers of protection. Find it. It is your responsibility. It is your privilege. It is your calling. Work your magic!

Conclusion

Before writing my final words, I would like to share with you a letter from a former student to his teacher. For the sake of anonymity, the names of both the teacher and the student have been changed.

Dear Mrs. Johnson,

It has been a long time, so you may not remember me. However, I doubt that you could ever forget me, as I made your life miserable for one solid year. I am writing for two reasons. One is to thank you for the profound influence that you had on my life. I am, believe it or not, a child psychologist, happily married with two beautiful children. And though I doubt that you realize it, you are the one person to whom I attribute my success. The second reason I'm writing is to apologize for my rotten behavior, stubbornness, and cruelty during the year that I spent in your classroom—a year that would turn my life around. You see, Mrs. Johnson, I was abused at home. Suffice it to say that my home life profoundly affected my personality, my behavior, and my self-concept. I had no control at home, so I tried to take control at school. The anger inside of me surfaced in my "lazy" appearance, and that same anger was directed at the most readily accessible adult—you. It always amazed me that no matter what I did or did not do, you never gave up on me. All of my other teachers were such easy targets. I controlled *them*. I forced them to lose their tempers, to fear my presence, and ultimately to give up on me. But you were different. The louder I got, the softer you became. Though you held me accountable for my actions, you managed to do that in such a dignified way. My stubbornness was no match for your infinite patience. My put-downs were defused with your put-ups. As hard as I tried to fail your class, you always found a way to make me succeed. I guess, in your quiet way, you understood that I definitely could not benefit from yet another aspect of failure in my life. I really tried to break you down. I needed to prove to myself that all adults could not be trusted. So, until the very end of school, I never gave up on trying to take you down. Likewise, you never gave up on trying to build me up. But because I probably left your classroom with my behavior looking much as it did on the first day I entered it, you probably thought you had not managed to reach me. But, oh, how wrong you were. Believe it or not, I respected you the moment you did not fight back.

I am not attempting to justify my actions. Rather, I simply want for you to know what a profound influence you had on my life. What a different place this world would be if all teachers treated all children the way you treated me. And what a wonderful place this world has become for me thanks to one person—you.

With inexpressible gratitude,
Jason Winslow

With that letter in mind, read carefully what I'm about to say to you, because if you do, you will be successful beyond your wildest imaginations. I say to you with the utmost sincerity and conviction that one person really *can* make a difference—and every one of you reading this is that person. There will be many "Jason Winslows" in your classes over the years. Sometimes they will be very easy to spot, but more often they will be very difficult to spot. Therefore, assume nothing. Do not give up on any student, and do not give in. Do not compromise your principles, do not lose faith, do not lose hope, do not lose your high expectations, and do *not* lose your temper. See through every bad behavior and into the good in every student you teach. Treat every student you encounter as Mrs. Johnson treated Jason Winslow, and you will be, in every sense of the word, a "teacher."

An Invitation for Your Comments

It has been my absolute pleasure to share this book with you. I eagerly invite your input, your suggestions, or any stories you would like to share for future editions of this book. Please feel free to contact me:

> Annette Breaux
> LaFourche Parish Schools
> 110 Bowie Road
> Thibodaux, LA 70301
> abreaux@eyeoneducation.com

You may also contact the publisher at:

> www.eyeoneducation.com